Called to Excellence

Heeth Varnedoe III

Heeth Varnedoe III
Phil 2V6

Evergreen
PRESS

Called to Excellence
by Heeth Varnedoe
Copyright ©2006 Heeth Varnedoe

ISBN 1-58169-199-8
For Worldwide Distribution
Printed in the U.S.A.

Evergreen Press
P.O. Box 191540 • Mobile, AL 36619
800-367-8203

TABLE OF CONTENTS

ACKNOWLEDGMENTS

Creston Nelson Morrill—in the early days of the original manuscript, she was a tremendous help in organizing the material.

Chip and Kim Mitchell—Kim's courage and love of the Lord was a tremendous witness to me and my wife.

Brian and Kathy Banashak—I appreciate Brian's guiding hand through the process of getting this book published, and Kathy and her tremendous ability to help incorporate the stories into the book.

My immediate family—Jacqueline and Robert, Elizabeth and Rand, Heeth and Susan, and Howard and Dawn—special thanks for all your encouragement throughout the writing of this book.

DEDICATION

To Jacqueline, my wife
of 46 years—a real prayer warrior
and source of encouragement.
You have truly been a light to me.

FOREWORD

Finally a book has been written on being successful based on the heart of heaven, which is mankind doing work on earth according to God's standard of excellence. The vital truths that Heeth presents in this book are not just from book learning but were derived from life experiences. They are in agreement with all great books on success and leadership, but more importantly they are in accordance with the greatest authority—the God who created man and placed him upon earth to work. In the Garden of Eden God commissioned man to do physical work by tending the Garden, and mental work by naming all the creatures that God had created for man. Mankind was commissioned to be productive (fruitful) and fill the earth with people doing their appointed work

Heeth Varnedoe has done an excellent job in presenting the principles to practice and the attributes to avoid in order to fulfill our call to excellence. I can verify that he has practiced these principles of excellence in all areas of his life After Heeth retired from his position as president of Flowers Foods, he served as president of Christian International Business Network. He helped us establish excellence in our ministry, which laid a good foundation for it to function with the favor of God. When Heeth taught in our conferences and seminars, his message always included his passion which was for us to do our work for God with excellence. He has developed the strong conviction and character of integrity, honesty and faithfulness with a high level of trustworthiness.

The truths are made known with many very interesting and enlightening life experiences and stories. One will have a hard time putting the book down until it is consumed. I am very proud of the excellent book he has made available to us. This book should be read by every worker regardless of their profession. I will make sure all my staff and employees receive a copy to read. It should definitely make them successful workers who will gain favor with God and man. The Bible says that it is a praise and honor to God when we do our work with excellence. We are all "Called to Excellence." God bless you, Heeth, for taking the time to show us how to fulfill that call.

—Dr. Bill Hamon
Apostle/Bishop of Christian International Ministries Network; Founder of Christian International Business Network; author of The Day of the Saints *and 8 other major books*

INTRODUCTION

By all outward appearances, I was a successful man when I was thirty-four. As a middle manager for Flowers Foods, I was rapidly climbing the corporate ladder and was headed for the top. I was an able provider for my family, had a nice home, a beautiful wife and four healthy children. I was even a church elder.

But all was not well behind the facade. At work, I had gained the reputation of being a tough taskmaster. Many of my subordinates responded to me out of fear rather than out of loyalty or respect. At home, my children craved my affection, but they were often disappointed. There was no fooling them; they knew that work was my top priority. As for my relationship with Jacqueline, my high school sweetheart and wife of 11 years, I had convinced myself that it would just take care of itself. Suffice it to say that nurturing was not a part of my vocabulary. The strain was starting to show. I came to a place where I realized that the way I was living was just not working.

Twenty-six years later, it was time to pursue a new venture. The journey of change I had begun from being a "successful" but miserable man to one who experienced a truly successful and happy life is nothing short of miraculous. I had been called to excellence when I was 34 in a way that was totally foreign to everything I believed as a hard-charging, bottom-line corporate climber.

You may be wondering whether my company suffered because I (and others in the organization) had committed my professional life to Christian principles. I think the financials speak for themselves. With the help of thousands of loyal and dedicated team members we saw Flowers Foods grow into a Fortune 500 company. But if you only look at the bottom line, you're missing the boat. My family too had been transformed along the way.

During my journey God has taught me many things, including a revolutionary (for me) way of seeking after success and helped me respond to His call to excellence in every aspect of my life. And I am truly grateful.

Lord, who may dwell in your sanctuary? Who may live on your holy hill?

He whose walk is blameless and who does what is righteous,

who speaks the truth from his heart and has no slander on his tongue,

who does his neighbour no wrong and casts no slur on his fellow man,

who despises a vile man but honours those who fear the Lord,

who keeps his oath even when it hurts,

who lends his money without usury

and does not accept a bribe against the innocent.

He who does these things will never be shaken.

—Psalm 15:1-5

CHAPTER ONE

Seeking After Success

Success—that place we all long for both privately and publicly—can be either an unattainable burden we carry with us all our lives or a wonderful experience that only gets better with time as we grow in it. The difference is determined by whether we understand what true success is and if we choose to pursue it.

Most of us aspire to be different as we head into adulthood. We look at the wrongs in the world and vow that we'll make them right. But after a few years, we tend to fall into line with the folks ahead of us, the ones who've become numb to the idea that there is a better way to live our lives. Very few people avoid the trap of mediocrity, but I sense with each passing day, more and more of us are looking for a way to free ourselves from it and pursue the success that God has had in mind for us all along.

Success is not determined by how much money we make, although we are usually financially rewarded by our success. Success is not determined by our innate talents, although they are gifts God has given us to use as tools along the way. Success cannot be defined by our social standing or our ranking in the corporate world, although many people attempt to define it that way. A janitor can be as successful as a CEO; an entrepreneur can be as successful as a corporate giant; a young mother can be as successful as a seasoned grandmother.

So then, what is success? Success, as I see it, is wholeheartedly pursuing God's call to excellence in whatever situation He has placed us, using whatever means and talents He has given us. Success is found in following God's will and God's ways in our lives—both professionally and personally.

In this book, we will deal primarily with our call to excellence in the business world and in our family life. These two facets of life really cannot be separated from one another, although people quite often mistakenly try to ignore one in order to become successful in the other. Both are intrinsic parts of our lives, however, and as such, are intertwined in bringing God's excellence into our world.

A Transcending Factor

One overriding factor that will determine how successful we become is our walk of faith. "Faith in business, you must be kidding," some may say. "I deal strictly with numbers, the bottom line is my guide." Others may not see how their faith can possibly make a difference in their family life. "The kids are teens, you just have to wait it out," they repeat over and over. Faith is the one factor that will make the ultimate difference between success or failure in life. (We must add at this point, however, that there are many people who are not Christians but have become powerful, wealthy people. How fulfilled they feel deep down is anyone's guess. How successful their families are is another matter altogether.)

Walking in faith enables a person to put everything else into perspective. You begin to realize that life is not just about you. In business you understand how many other people are involved in the decisions you make—those involved with the production, distribution, and consumption of goods and services. In other words, you begin to get a larger picture that's it not just your little world in which you can maneuver with blinders on, seeing nothing but what is in front of you.

You begin to see that your job, your company, your corporation is important because it affects the lives of many people you may never even know. You can get a glimpse of this bigger picture through God's perspective by developing a relationship with Him and reading His Word. When you walk in faith, keeping your focus on God and adhering to His value system, you are equipped to make business decisions in an excellent way that leads to success both for you and for the people around you.

In family life, it's the same way. After I became a Christian, I began to work at making changes in my relationships with my four kids. I saw that I needed to help them grow by seeking God's direction for their lives. It's so easy to put a guilt complex on a child when you think you are disciplining them. We need to help them grow, stand with them as they go through various learning experiences, and keep our focus on God to give them what they need. Each one of my four kids is different, and I had to learn how to develop their value system so that their perspective was enlarged beyond themselves. I needed to help them find their own vision for who God created them to be.

It's easy to put impossible demands on our children. For example, my four kids have different scholastic abilities. I could have told one of them that he needed to make the same grades as his sister, but that would have put him in bondage. It wouldn't have been impossible for him to accomplish, but it would have put a pressure on him that wasn't necessary. As a result of giving him the freedom to be himself, on his own initiative, he set aside his idea of playing football after he graduated from high school because it did not fit in with the goals he saw for his life.

None of this change in mindset happens overnight. The road to success and to excellence is a winding one that takes us through many rocky places, over many raging rivers, and through many storms, but if we persevere toward the goal and seek to learn from others and listen to God's voice, we will always find the next destination is one we look forward to with joy.

The Bullseye

As we have seen, success is defined by how we use our God-given gifts and talents and our willingness to respond to God's call on our lives. It is about everything we are as a man or a woman in every aspect of our lives.

A good example of a successful man who made

a difference in many people's lives through his pursuit of excellence is George Washington Carver. He was a brilliant man. His work with peanuts became so well known nationally that automotive giant Henry Ford tried to hire him. He offered Carver big money to chuck the peanut industry and help him in the emerging automobile business. But Carver felt that he had a calling, so he declined the offer. Over the course of his career he came up with hundreds of ways to use the peanut, and his research helped to revolutionize agricultural practices in the South.

When God calls us, it may be on the peanut level—dealing with something that, at first glance, looks inconsequential, but the end result is something much more significant. We need to be careful not to ignore His calling just because, on the surface, it looks insignificant.

Success or failure of a person is not measured in a moment or a day. It is measured over a lifetime. In the grand scheme of things, we are only here on earth for a flick of a second, but what we do while we are here is critically important. The fact is that we can't be successful until we take the time to reflect on where our gifts lie. We can make a boatload of money and still not succeed if we've failed to use our God-given abilities and function in fulfilling God's will for our lives.

The Talents

There are familiar stories in the New Testament called parables, which were one of Christ's chosen methods of communicating a message. These stories share familiar scenes with the people of their day: the farmer scattering the seed; the pearl merchant who was always on the lookout for choice pearls; the shepherd who lost one of his 100 sheep; the vineyard workers who were paid a full day's wages regardless of the number of hours they put in. In Jesus' time, people understood farming, fishing, shepherding, and working the vineyards. They celebrated wedding feasts and could easily relate to the story of the prodigal son or the faithful servant.

In the parable of the talents, located in Matthew 25:14-30, a wealthy man, who was about to go on a trip, called his servants together and gave them money to invest for him while he was gone. He gave five talents to one, two talents to another, and one talent to the last. The key here is that he divided it according to their abilities. The servant who received the five talents of gold really went to work and soon doubled it. He must have wheeled and dealed up a storm. I'd love to know how he did it! The second servant also went to work and doubled his money. But the servant with the one talent of gold dug a hole in the ground and buried it for safekeeping.

When their master returned, he called in the servants for an accounting. The first two won accolades and were promoted. But he was not pleased with the third fellow. "You could at least have put the money in the bank so it could have earned some interest," the master said in exasperation. He ordered the shirker's one talent of gold be given to the servant who had started out with the most gold. "To those who use well what they are given, even more will be given and they will have an abundance" (Matt. 25:29).

This parable puts everyone on a level playing field. It doesn't matter how smart someone is, the fact that one outranks another, or even that someone makes more money than someone else. All that matters, it says, is that you and I both are doing our level best to fully use the gifts and talents that God has given us.

What a challenge—"give it all we got" every day in every way we can! And it is not just about our performance in the corporate world. No matter how fancy our title is or how important some people think we are, we're not successful if our family life is falling apart. (We'll cover that more fully in a later chapter.)

God has not designed us to be wimps, sitting on the sidelines of life, wringing our hands over what our lot in life has handed us. Nor does He desire us to be so driven by our responsibilities that we leave no room for our faith to grow and our relationship with Him to prosper. No, He has a specific job and purpose for us to accomplish—and possibly more than one over a lifetime—so that our lives would reflect His glory and not our own.

After 40 years in the corporate life, I can see these truths played out in situation after situation, time after time in a career that began in an inauspicious way.

Starting at the Bottom

I began my journey in business by working summers at Flowers Foods, sweeping the floors, changing oil in delivery trucks and doing pretty much anything I was asked to do. My limited idea of success at that time was to earn some needed money. Little did I know that one day I would be part of the management team that had the responsibility for the leadership of a Fortune 500 company. When I began my career at Flowers, it consisted of only two bakeries, one in Thomasville, Georgia, and one in Jacksonville, Florida. It was strictly a small-town family business.

During the summer before my freshman year of college, I was given an opportunity for a real job in the company: driving a bread route as a substitute for vacationing salesmen. I received one week's training from an experienced salesman and then I was on my own. I'll never forget how excited I was the night before I made my first solo run.

That first day was one of the worst of my life. I spent most of the time getting lost, and when I finally arrived at each of my destinations, there always seemed to be some confusion about what it was that I was supposed to be delivering. I thought the day would never end. When I laid my head on my pillow that night, I just knew there was no way I could drag myself out of bed at 2 a.m. to report to work the next day, but report to work I did.

I learned many things that summer. While I didn't realize it at the time, I was, in effect, running my own small business as I serviced my route. The self-discipline I gained in learning how to manage my time to take care of all my accounts was the first key step I took toward experiencing success. It would be a real asset in later years as I progressed through the ranks of management.

Running those vacation bread routes took me all over the south Georgia area. As a salesman, I was responsible for everything I put on the truck. I had to write up sales tickets and put in orders for the following week plus a lot of other book work.

Just before my graduation from college, I was

invited to work for Flowers Foods on a permanent basis. Despite the fact that my mother was related to the Flowers, it was made quite clear to me that I'd be starting out on the bottom rung. (Mother was not a common stockholder nor did she hold any position in the company.) Years later, at my retirement party, Mr. Flowers recounted the conversation in which he had told me that in order to be respected in the company I would have to give 25-30% more than my peers. So I added "gaining respect" to my idea of success.

I had no idea when I first accepted the job offer that I'd become a "company man." While I knew that I wanted to move up to the next level and get off the bread route, I was still a man with a warped vision when it came to the bigger picture of career and family.

I took over a bread route in Bainbridge, Georgia, right after Christmas that year. The next March, Jacqueline and I married and had a wonderful one-week honeymoon at Hilton Head, a generous wedding gift which we truly appreciated. After the honeymoon we drove to Jacksonville, which was to be our new home and the location of my new route. When I called my boss, Jerry Bussell, to find out the details of starting my new job, he told me I was to be at the loading platform in Jacksonville at 2 a.m. the next day. I assumed that this very early start must be so we could discuss the particulars of my assignment over breakfast. When I showed up that morning, there was no breakfast or discussion. I was simply told to get to work. It turned out that my new boss was a former Marine who had fought at Iwo Jima! Although that introduction to Jerry showed me his no-nonsense side, I also soon learned that he never asked anything of others that he was not willing to do himself. Over the years Jerry would play a major role in the company's growth in the Florida market.

A route salesman's job is demanding work. I worked six, sometimes seven days a week, loading and unloading the truck, keeping track of sales and driving from stop to stop on my route. After six months, I was transferred to a route in Albany, Georgia. Six months later I was transferred again, and we packed up and moved to Dothan, Alabama, which I later learned was one of the toughest markets Flowers had at the time.

Although the various courses required for my business degree were a good framework for understanding the corporate world, they did not fully prepare me for the day-to-day challenges of modern day business. I had to learn many things through observation and experience.

I learned that if you are responsible with what's given to you, you will advance and be given more responsibility. When you learn discipline in one area, it spills over or strengthens other areas that also need discipline. For example it took a lot of discipline for me when I was an 18 year old to get up at 2:30 and 3 o'clock in the morning to run the bread routes, although it's not that big of a deal. I've seen young people eagerly get up early in the morning to go hunting, but going to work early can be a challenge at that age. I was learning the discipline needed to be responsible for getting baked products into these grocery stores.

There was one extremely difficult route that took an enormous amount of energy and planning to do successfully. It was, in effect, like running a four-minute mile. It had the reputation as being the biggest and toughest route in Flowers Foods. If I had been put on that route the very first time I went out, it probably would have broken my back. Our company understood the principle of management that says not to push people too fast and too far, or they burn out. Thank goodness, somebody had enough sense to let me get the easier routes under my belt before they assigned me to the most challenging one.

Being Accountable

One of the most significant principles I learned about success through these early years was the importance of being accountable, i.e., taking responsibility for my actions in both big and small matters. For example, in the early days of my tenure as a route salesman, I failed to service an account one day. When I discovered my mistake at the end of the route, I decided not to backtrack to the business (a restaurant) but to just apologize on the next day's delivery. I assumed the customer would understand and not think much of it. Was I dead wrong! When I arrived the next day, I found that the business had already replaced me with another supplier.

Route salesmen are responsible for everything they put on their truck. When they return at night, if they don't have either the money for the merchandise or any undelivered product, they must put in their own money to make up for any shortfall. My customers were depending on me to show up on time and with what they needed.

Experiences like this helped me to become more disciplined and accountable, two traits which would be especially important as I moved higher in the ranks of management, heading toward my success!

After three incredibly hard years during which I supervised a half dozen or so routes, I was appointed sales manager at the cake plant in Thomasville, and, three years later, named director of sales. I was on my way to a better life! I was respected now. But I was a driven and unhappy man!

CHAPTER TWO

The Wrong Compass

The world prepares us to look at the bottom line and gauge our success by handing us a compass for our lives with the needle always pointing to "M" for money to show us the way.

For the first eleven years of our marriage, and through the birth and early years of our four children, my goals were to get ahead in the business world in order to provide the necessities for my family. However, the critical importance of being a fully engaged husband and father never crossed my mind. To my way of thinking, necessities were material things: a house, clothes, cars, and food on the table. We attended church most Sundays and I eventually assumed a leadership role there, but I put about as much thought and energy into that role as I did my family life.

In January of 1971, by all outward appearances, I was on top of the world. In fact, although I hated to admit it, I was running on empty.

I began asking myself questions: *If everything about my life looks so good to the people on the outside looking in, how can I feel so empty? What am I doing wrong? How have things gotten to this point? How can I fix it?*

Most of us experience a wake-up call at some point in our life. For some, it's the birth of a child. For others it's the death of a friend or loved one. But for all of us, it is the realization that the way we are doing things isn't working. For me, it was the absolute certainty that I was about to lose my family. It wasn't that Jacqueline was going to leave me—it was that I had already left her and the kids. We occupied the same house, but we didn't live together. I was too busy.

I didn't have a Ph.D. in psychology, but I did have enough sense to know that I was at a crossroads in my life with my family. And at that point I had two choices: I could bury my head in the sand or I could start finding out what I needed to be doing differently. Knowing just how stubborn I was, God began to bring people I could relate to across my path. And they just happened to be Christians.

A Close Encounter

One day, Jacqueline told me that she had experienced a close encounter with "the Lord." I thought, *Good for her!* It did seem a bit out of the ordinary, but I was really too busy to give it much thought.

A friend had invited Jacqueline over to her home to share her life story, her struggles, and how she had committed her life to God. The changes that had resulted in this woman's life made a deep impression on Jacqueline, who came home and made a decision to recommit her life to God.

I was out of town when Jacqueline met with this friend and subsequently made her decision. When I returned two days later she told me, "You'll never guess what happened to me!" At first I thought she had wrecked the car. Instead she told me that she had recommitted her life to God and now had the most wonderful peace. At the time I thought to myself, *All she needs is a good night's sleep.* But not only did this experience have a lasting effect, the changes I came to see in her life were all for the good!

The New Testament passage that talks about

our being the light of the world reminds me of
Jacqueline and how God placed her in my life to
lead me to Himself.

*You are the light of the world like a city on a
mountain, glowing in the night for all to
see...let it shine for all to see, so that everyone
will praise your heavenly Father* (Matt. 5:14).

Over the period of a year, I began to see a tremendous change in my wife. Jacqueline became fulfilled in her life, but I didn't have a clue how to
begin to do so in mine.

As my wife began hosting church-related meetings at our home, some of those clues showed up
right in my own living room. One of these people
was Russell Linenkohl, then a manager with
General Electric in Jacksonville. So many people
turned out to hear him tell about his life experiences that I had to sit in a hallway just outside the
den in order to hear him. Russell was a businessman, who by all outward appearances seemed
to be what I considered "normal." He certainly
spoke my language. However, as with others I'd
met of late through these events, there was something different about him. While I couldn't put my
finger on it, I began to sense that my life was
missing something extremely important.

Like the student that I've always been when it
came to business matters, I started reading anything I could lay my hands on about family and

religion. One of the best books I read was *The Christian Family* by Larry Christianson. It had a profound effect on me as far as my responsibility to my wife and my kids.

It wasn't a particularly emotional time for me as I went through the process of opening myself up for introspection. But I arrived at the conclusion that this wasn't something I could fix on my own. But where could I turn for help?

The First Order of Business

A long-time friend, Jim Armstrong, is the kind of guy you can count on for solid advice. During World War II, he was shot down over France and made it back to England with the help of the French underground. He's as real a person as I know. He also happened to be a Presbyterian minister. I called and asked if I could talk with him.

I will never forget walking into Jim's office that Saturday. I never felt happier in my life to see a friendly face. By this time I was thoroughly confused about the emptiness I was feeling. Over the course of an hour or so, I poured out my doubts about who I was, who I wanted to be, and how to get there. I told him that for the first time in my adult life I was at a complete loss as to where I was headed. I confessed, "The way I'm living life is not working. I'm successful in the business world but not with my family." That's when he asked me that extraordinarily simple question, "Are you saved? Are you a born again Christian?" I told Jim that I really didn't know.

Up to that time, my concept of being saved had involved some sort of rescue effort connected to an accident or natural disaster, as in, "Some of the passengers on the Titanic made it into lifeboats and were saved by rescue ships." Or, in football, where a defender tips a last-chance pass away from the receiver, preventing a game-winning touchdown, thereby saving the game. The only time I'd heard the word used in the context of religion was when I'd come across some evangelist on television talking about being saved. Needless to say, I hadn't paid much attention.

After months of soul searching, I still had only a vague idea what Jim was asking me. "Being saved is the first order of business," said Jim. A light bulb went on in my head. Now this I could relate to.

Then he asked if he could pray with me. As Jim led me in a prayer for salvation, I felt that my world as I knew it was being turned on its head. I could feel something happening—something powerful. And while I didn't fall to the floor or have a vision, when Jim stopped praying I knew I was a different person. I left his office feeling as though the weight of the world had been lifted off me and wondered, *What do I do now?* When I asked Jim this question, without hesitation, he responded, "The first step is to start reading the Bible, beginning with the Gospel of John. If you're going to become like someone, you must get to know them. John's Gospel gives us a wonderful picture of Christ and helps us to understand who He is."

I thought that everyone would immediately take notice of the new me. *I'm different,* I thought. *I'm a Christian!* My life was now very exciting so surely the world must be a different place. I had a rude awakening, though, when I drove home in the same car to the same house to the same family and, on Monday, to the same job and discovered that most things hadn't changed. This wasn't quite what I'd expected. I didn't stop to think that my success in business hadn't happened overnight. I had progressed step by step up the corporate ladder, although now I wasn't sure it was the right ladder. No doubt about it, I still felt called to my job, but there are various ladders we can climb that are on different sides of the same top. Which view did I want when I was up there? Was it a ladder that only held me or was it one that held my family and church life too?

So there I was. I was saved. And I had to ask myself, *Now what?* When the answer came, it was clear that I had my work cut out for me. The bottom line is that once you become a Christian, you need to begin to change your lifestyle. You try to live your life the way Jesus did. Anyone can be saved, but the real challenge lies in transforming your life so that you become the person that God made you to be.

The road to holiness is not paved with gold and silver. It can be downright muddy. There are potholes and detours. There are dead ends. There are so many choices. This is the real world, after all. So how do we find our way?

There are volumes of books that have been written that tell us how to grow our businesses or to grow individually in our respective vocations. We don't accomplish this by sitting idly by. We do our homework. We read the *Wall Street Journal* and the trades. We attend conferences. We network. From the time I went to work for Flowers in the 1960s until I retired in 1997 I never stopped learning.

I soon realized that the same holds true when we start our Christian walk. I had to begin my journey by studying the Bible and learning from others farther along the way than I was. I had to adapt myself to effectively live out my faith in the changing world around me. Just like a baby continually learns to adapt and become effective in the physical world, I had undergone a spiritual rebirth and began a lifelong process of renewing my mind to discern what God's will was for me in each circumstance. I had to continually resist the pull to be conformed to the world and instead be in tune with my heavenly Father. There is a tremendous conflict between the competing perspective of God's value system versus the world's value system.

It may seem contradictory to suggest that obedience wins freedom, but I truly believe that obedience to God is the only way we can free ourselves from our past, our bad habits, and our old way of life. But we can't be obedient to God if we don't know the rules and if we don't know Him. And that is where many of us stumble. We make it much more difficult than it really is.

The Beginning of a New Climb

Little by little I began to see that with true success comes the peace we have when we know we are in harmony with the purpose that God created us for. It begins by opening ourselves completely to Him, holding nothing back. We put ourselves completely in His care and trust the sacrifice of His Son to cover our ugly and self-centered flaws.

I have a farm in Pavo, Georgia, about 20 miles outside Thomasville. In 1997, I planted a section of pine trees. A year later, the "live rate" was 10 percent. In other words, 90 percent of the trees died. That simply was not acceptable, so I did what any good businessman would do. I brought in experts to tell me where I'd gone wrong. The diagnosis: bad trees. The following year, I planted trees again. The live rate held at 10 percent. So I called the experts back in. Same experts, new diagnosis: lack of rain.

The next year it came time to plant once again, and I thought I'd give it one more try. I had a new man operating the tractor that turns the ground and plants the seedlings. I just happened to be there when he started plowing. He went down the first row and came to a dead stop. He cut the engine and walked over to me. "Heeth," he said, "you have a major problem here. These trees are going to die." I asked him what he thought the problem was. "You've got a hard pan," he said.

A hard pan, he explained, is a layer of extremely hard ground that lies beneath the surface soil. It's like concrete. It's also very deceptive since the soil on top looks pretty good. The trees had looked great when they went into the ground and they had looked great as spring began to come on, but as the season progressed, they had almost all died. There was no place for the roots to go, there was no place for them to reach down and grab the nourishment they needed. He said we needed to bring in a subplow to go deep and break it up. So we got a big plow and went down 24 inches. After we'd broken up the hard pan, we planted the trees. The live rate that year was 95 percent.

I realized that in beginning my journey as a Christian, my heart was like that hard pan. I don't mind telling you that in my case, plowing new spiritual ground required a backhoe. My foundational structure was all wrong. All the old mindsets were still there and had to be torn down. It began to be clear to me that I must live by God's value system, not man's.

God began to reveal this and other things to me through the Scriptures. Bible verses started to take on new meaning to me as He showed me how they were applicable specifically to me, not just the ancients of biblical times. As a natural early riser, I found that this was the best time of day for me to spend with Him and His Word. One of the verses that spoke to me about my hard ground is in Hosea 10:12,

> *Plant the good seeds of righteousness and you will reap a crop of my love; plow the hard ground of your hearts, for now is the time to seek the Lord, that he may come and shower salvation upon you.*

Discovering new spiritual truths was exciting, but like a neophyte in any discipline, my zeal for new found truths often outran my maturity in understanding how to apply them. I was not prone to really listen to others during this period and would cut people off in conversations. I became legalistic about the Christian life as I quickly set aside the grace that had gently brought me to salvation.

This attitude soon became evident in my relationship with my oldest daughter, Jacqueline. One day as we were taking one of our regular walks, I began talking to her about being a woman of excellence. Suddenly she turned to me with tears in her eyes. I congratulated myself, *Heeth, you have really made an impact with your daughter!* She soon burst my bubble when she said, "Daddy, you didn't hear a word I was saying!" That was a real wake-up call. I had not really been listening to my children, especially to their heart. God began to show me the wonderful uniqueness of my children with their different personalities and gifts. But this didn't happen until I began to truly listen to them. Then, as in other tough times in family and other settings, God's grace was the healing tonic to bring peace and a reason for hope again.

As I began to grow in my faith, my priorities changed. Things that were once very important to me were no longer significant, and new things began to take their place. In particular, I began to devote my leisure time to my family—taking walks, cooking out, and just enjoying being together.

When you are working long hours, you need to

spend quality time with your kids. In order to make that time, I gave up my extracurricular activities. I used to play golf and I quit because I just couldn't do that and be with them too. I used to go to Georgia football games on Saturday, and I found that I had to quit doing that when I began to prioritize my time to include my family. There wasn't anything intrinsically wrong with those activities, I just did not have time for them during that season of my life because I wanted to make time for my family.

Due to my new commitment to family time, we also became less available for social activities in which we were formerly involved. I experienced joy in my relationship with Jacqueline and our children because it was now based on God's love and not how we were feeling or how our day had gone. The journey that we all embarked on saw our values change, which brought about a sense of victory and peace in my life like nothing I had ever known. This was evident in many things, but in particular in my discipline of the children which was now rooted in love and not fear.

Thomasville is a small town today. It was even smaller in the early 70s when I became a Christian. Word quickly got around that Jacqueline and I had "gone over the edge." We had moved from a mainline denominational church to a smaller church of the same denomination, and then began attending a house church (a small group of worshippers meeting in one of the member's homes), which I'm sure was threatening to a lot of people. Jacqueline and I were not always wise in the way we presented our new-found passion for the Lord to our family and friends. I'm quite certain some folks thought we'd run off and joined a cult.

One day, W.H. Flowers, our board chairman, called me into his office. He was known as "The Man." "I'm real concerned," he said. "You're a key man in this organization, but I can't have any religious fanatics running around." Mr. Flowers suggested that Jacqueline and I just "calm down" a little bit.

I know now that he had a legitimate concern that I would become so completely wrapped up in religion I would let my work slide. As a manager, I've seen it happen to others over the years. At the time I was really nervous. I loved my job and I needed a paycheck. Yet I knew that what was happening to me was real and that I did not want to compromise my beliefs. I simply couldn't back off from what God had told me to do. I explained this to Mr. Flowers and added, "If I ever do anything to embarrass you, or if I ever don't do what I'm supposed to do on the job, I'll leave." This was my way of letting him know that even though I felt compelled to be bold in my faith that I intended to do it with wisdom. I think that is what he was trying to tell me he wanted also. And that's where we left it. He never mentioned it again.

So I had a new mind-set to grasp and a new way to live. As in business you never quit learning if you want to be successful.

Obedience

There's a word—obedience—that's not an easy part of most people's vocabulary. Those of us in management are used to giving the orders. But if we are going to be truly successful, we have to make that word active in our lives. We have to play by the rules—ours and God's. His rules are laid out in the Bible.

When I became a Christian, I felt that God had called me to change, to be different, to start incorporating His value system into my life. When we start walking in obedience, we can stop worrying about that next promotion. When we are doing what God is asking of us, He's going to do the promoting.

In his letter to the people of Ephesus, Paul wrote,

> For it is by grace that you have been saved (from your transgressions and sins) through faith…not by works, so that no one can boast. For we are God's workmanship, created in Christ Jesus to do good works, which God prepared in advance for us to do (Eph. 2:8-10 NIV).

As Christians, we don't get to take the credit for our good works! They are His, not ours. And in the final analysis, it's not about the works—it's about our faithfulness in pursuing them.

Once we have done that, Christ frees us to serve Him. We no longer are burdened by the need to please other men or satisfy our own idea of who we think we should be. All we have to do is focus on pleasing Him, and we do that by allowing Him to live in us through His Spirit and His Word. We spend time reading the Bible, praying and listening to hear what God has to say to us, and then responding to His guidance. At the end of our journey, we will receive that most valued of all accolades of success—our Lord and Saviour saying to us, "Well done, my good and faithful servant. Come and share your master's happiness" (Matt. 25:21 NIV).

We are constantly tested in our vocations. Our performance is reviewed. How are we doing? What do we need to do to improve our results? When is our next promotion coming? In the marketplace, we turn to our boss for answers. If we own our own business, we look at the profit and loss statement. As Christians, the acid test is our desire to obey His Word and to live our lives as Jesus wants us to do.

As a nation and as a society, we are results oriented. Over the past 32 years, I have been on a mission in which the results of my life are Jesus-based. No, I haven't arrived. But that's what the cross is all about. There is no condemnation of those who are in Christ Jesus.

When it comes to our Christian walk, we are either going forward or backward. There is no middle ground. As Christians we are motivated to grow and learn. His power and direction in our lives always should be on the rise.

I can tell you that fearing God and obeying His commands is a tall order for anyone. It is a never ceasing struggle, regardless of our vocation. Through my experience, I've come to the conclusion that there are two fundamentals we must understand: the significance of the cross and the necessity of growing in our love and knowledge of Jesus Christ.

CHAPTER THREE

Learning Trust

Business leaders are by their very nature "fix-it" people. Got a cash flow problem? Fix it. Your plant's production falls below standard? Fix it. You have a key employee who's not carrying his weight? Fix it. Your spouse thinks you need to spend more time with your family? By golly, try to fix it. Most of us are born this way, and it's the way we live. We don't know any other way. From sunup on Monday through sundown on Saturday, at the very least, we are in control.

But sooner or later, a situation will arise that we can't fix. Something will happen that is absolutely out of our control. We have to totally trust God.

I have an 11-year-old grandson named Rand. He's the deep thinker of the family and very creative. He spends hours building with legos. In December 2001, Rand and his older brother David were riding on the back of a trailer that was carrying a heavy farming tractor. They were having a great time. In an instant, all that changed.

Rand's blue jeans got caught on the wheel of the trailer. Before he could say anything, he was pulled beneath it. The wheels ran over him diagonally, from just below his knee on one side and across the shoulder on the other. The weight crushed his ribs, lungs, and shoulder, and the wheels narrowly missed his head. As a result, he had massive internal injuries.

My son-in-law, a physician, and his father witnessed the accident and quickly called 911, but it was clear that time was working against Rand. Moments later, my daughter Elizabeth drove up to the scene of the accident. Once Rand's dad determined that his neck wasn't broken, he loaded him into the family car. On the way to the hospital he worked to save him. Rand stopped breathing, but his dad revived him. During the trip to the hospital, Elizabeth prayed for Rand's survival as she held him in her arms.

Once they arrived at the hospital, Rand was

placed on life support. The doctor said that his lungs might be damaged beyond repair. It would be 48-72 hours before we would know whether he would survive.

Jacqueline and I were out of town at the time and rushed back to Tallahassee where they had placed him in the pediatric intensive care unit. In the meantime, word went out worldwide via the Internet that Rand was in need of prayer. People all around the world began praying for him. It was awesome. Of course, it didn't take long for word of the accident to spread across town either. It seemed as though everyone in Thomasville was praying for Rand.

The next morning, Jacqueline and I went back to the hospital. It was then that my daughter-in-law, Susan, spoke the words that pierced my heart like a dagger. "Big Heeth," she said, "You cannot fix this."

That night, after returning from the hospital, I could not sleep so I went to the Lord in prayer. "Lord, I just really want him to live," I said, "but he's in Your hands. I trust You."

Later, as I was sitting in my office, God spoke to me. I heard His voice. It was as clear as the sky is blue. He said, "Read Psalm 30."

I will praise you, Lord, for you have rescued me. You refused to let my enemies triumph over

*me. O Lord my God, I cried out to you for help,
and you restored my health. You brought me up
from the grave, O Lord. You kept me from
falling into the pit of death* (Psalm 30:1-3).

After I read this psalm, I felt a wave of relief
wash over me. At that moment, I knew with a certainty that Rand would survive. But bringing Rand
back from death's door required a team effort. The
family members and friends on the team prayed
their hearts out for him. The rest of the team—
the doctors and nurses, the respiratory specialists,
the engineers who designed the equipment used
during his hospital stay, the medical researchers
who formulated the antibiotics that fought off in-
fection—used their God-given gifts, callings and
talents to keep our grandson alive.

There is no question in my mind that God
could have instantly healed Rand had He chosen
to do so. But that was not His choice. Prayer,
working in conjunction with the talents of many
dedicated professionals, delivered our miracle.
Without this powerful healing combination, Rand
would not be alive today.

Today, Rand is back to his old self, physically.
Yet I'm certain that he'll never be the same spiri-
tually. He and God have developed a very special
relationship. I will be forever grateful that his life
was spared.

In 2002 my dear wife Jacqueline was scheduled for routine outpatient surgery in Tallahassee. As an extra precaution the surgeon asked that we stay in town that evening after the operation rather than travel back to Thomasville. Upon being released from the hospital around 4:00 pm we checked into a local hotel to settle down and rest for the night. As time passed we began to realize that something was wrong and decided to return to the hospital. On examination the doctors discovered that Jacqueline had developed a hematoma which required more surgery and eventually resulted in her being put on life support. God worked through the prayers of many people and the skilled hands of the surgeon to bring Jacqueline back to full recovery.

In 2003 I was diagnosed with prostate cancer. After the doctor told me I had cancer, I didn't hear another word he said. First came a period of denial. Then came the hard realization that Heeth could do nothing himself to defeat this illness. I was not in control. I would have to depend on God and the medical community. Through many prayers and the surgical skills of Dr. Frey Marshall at Emory University, I am now cancer free!

I share these stories with you because it is important for us "Type A's" to know that there are some things we just can't fix.

Giving Up Control

Giving up some degree of control was a significant challenge for me, not just in our family life, but particularly in business. One of the least endearing qualities of a control freak is his inability to let go. We'd sooner walk barefoot over hot coals. A lot of the unwillingness to surrender control stems from our own insecurities. It's hard to admit this, but I think there's a degree of jealousy involved. On some level we find other people's success threatening. But in the long term, you just can't run a successful business that way.

As I changed, the whole atmosphere of our company meetings changed. We didn't sit around holding hands singing Kumbaya, and we didn't hold prayer meetings, but things were different. That demonstrates the fact that not everyone who experiences a profound growth in their relationship with God needs to go to seminary or into the mission field. As Christians, those of us in business are called to full-time marketplace ministry. What greater place than the marketplace to have a servant's mentality? If we ever forget that we are here to serve, we are greatly diminished.

God called the apostle Paul to go to Rome. That wasn't exactly the cradle of Christianity. But while Paul was there, he wrote several of the epistles that, through the centuries, have been read by hundreds of millions of people around the world. Peter was a fisherman with a fleet of boats, yet God called him to walk with Jesus. After Jesus' death, Peter spent more than 30 years spreading the gospel. God gave him an assignment and he went out and completed it. I believe that Peter and his family accomplished all of this while remaining in the family fishing business.

God puts each of us where He needs us most. He's after ordinary people to do extraordinary things. By His mighty power at work within us, He is able to accomplish infinitely more than we would ever dare to ask or hope. When God calls us, we have to be humble enough to take the call.

Your attitude should be the same that Christ Jesus had. Though He was God, He did not demand and cling to his rights as God. He made himself nothing; He took the humble position of a slave and appeared in human form. And in human form He obediently humbled himself even further by dying a criminal's death on the cross (Phil. 2:6-8).

As Christians we must discipline ourselves to serve as God calls us, not at our convenience, but as He would have us do. Oswald Chambers, the great preacher, teacher and missionary wrote that, from a human standpoint, it is far easier to serve God when we do not have a vision or a calling.

You may be more prosperous and successful

from the world's perspective, and will have more leisure time, if you never acknowledge the call of God. But once you receive a commission from Jesus Christ, the memory of what God asks of you will always be there to prod you on to do His will. You will no longer be able to work for Him on the basis of common sense *(My Utmost for His Highest)*.

Chambers argued that our ordinary and reasonable service to God may actually compete against our total surrender to Him. When we remind ourselves of how useful we are being, Chambers says that we

...(choose) our own judgment, instead of Jesus Christ to be our guide as to where we should go and where we could be used the most. Never consider whether or not you are of use—but always consider that you are not your own *(My Utmost for His Highest)*.

Once we receive a commission from Jesus Christ, we will no longer be able to work for Him solely on the common sense basis we are accustomed to operating within in the business world.

Different Outcomes

In the U.S., we are not used to failure. By 1970, the Apollo moon missions had become so routine that the television networks had significantly cut back their coverage. There was a sense that we were in control. Technology was our new god. Then, on Apollo 13, technology failed us.

Jerry Woodfill was the Warning System Engineer at Mission Control in Houston on April 13, 1970. His system was the first to alert mission control to any life-threatening malfunction aboard the spacecraft. He remembers the outpouring of prayer across the nation as he and others at mission control frantically sought solutions to the problems that threatened the lives of three astronauts.

Woodfill notes on his website that it was duct tape that saved them. "But why was duct tape stowed on board? Why did someone conceive of using it?" he writes. "Like Esther and her people, Jim Lovell and his crew benefited from favor from the same One who acted in millenniums past."

When all was said and done, a bunch of engineers and rocket scientists used their God-given intellect and skills to do everything they could to fix the problem. Then they had to give it up to God.

I've been in situations where I tried to fix a problem and it all blew up around me. Over the years, I've found myself in many situations that, on the surface, could not be fixed. I learned to pray and commit them to the Lord.

It's important to note that "fixing it" doesn't always result in the outcome we were aiming for. For example, at Flowers, sometimes we were in markets from which we had to extricate ourselves. In those instances, pulling out of the market was the fix. The outcome we are expecting doesn't always coincide with God's expected outcome.

There are some things that are simply out of our hands. When we have done everything we know to do personally and professionally, we have to turn things over to God. He will not fail us.

Some have argued that if there really is a God, He failed the United States on 9/11. Yet many who lost loved ones that day say that their faith in God remains unshaken. Lisa Beamer's husband, Todd, was one of those who tried to wrest back control from the hijackers on United Flight 93, which crashed in a field in rural Pennsylvania. She says that the key to her survival is that her faith wasn't rooted in governments, religion, tall buildings or frail people. "My faith and my security were in God," she says.

In her book, *Let's Roll,* Beamer writes that she struggled for days to deal with the shock of losing her husband coupled with the grief shared by the rest of the nation over the senseless and overwhelming loss of life inflicted by the terrorists. "And yet, in that dark moment of my soul, I first cried out to God. I knew without a doubt that my hope wasn't based on Todd or any other human being. Nor was it based even on life itself, when it got right down to it," she writes. "A thought struck me. Who are you to question God and say that you have a better plan than He does? You don't have the same wisdom and knowledge that He has, or the understanding of the big picture."

After attending a largely secular memorial service for those killed aboard Flight 93, Beamer writes that it struck her how hopeless the world is when God is factored out of the equation. "I don't think Todd chose to die, but he did choose for God's will to be done in his life. Knowing that, he stepped into the aisle of that plane, trusting by faith that regardless of what happened, God would be true to His Word. Before he took that first step, Todd knew where he was going, even if he should die. He had built his life on a firm foundation."

The week prior to the attack, Lisa Beamer had been preparing to teach a Bible study. She was referred by the study guide to a "memory verse." It turned out that the biblical passage was one that she had turned to for strength after the death of her father. Weeks after the attack, she learned that the scripture memorization card at the top of a stack that Todd had been studying daily while driving contained the very same verse from Romans.

Oh, what a wonderful God we have! How

*great are His riches and wisdom and knowl-
edge! How impossible it is for us to understand His decisions and His methods! For who
can know what the Lord is thinking? Who
knows enough to be His counselor? And who
could ever give Him so much that He would
have to pay it back? For everything comes
from Him; everything exists by His power and
is intended for His glory. To Him be the glory
evermore* (Rom. 11:33-36).

Our real character is revealed during those
times when we can't fix things. In Philippians,
Paul writes,

*Don't worry about anything; instead, pray
about everything. Tell God what you need, and
thank Him for all that He has done. If you do
this, you will experience God's peace, which is
far more wonderful than the human mind can
understand. His peace will guard your hearts
and minds as you live in Christ Jesus* (Phil.
4:6-7).

Prayer has been a tremendous source of
strength for me during trying times. I turned to
one prayer again and again when I found myself
facing a particularly difficult decision: Let the
darkness be brought into the light.

Just because we are Christians, it doesn't
mean that we will never fail. It's how we deal with
failure that sets us apart.

CHAPTER FOUR

Business—God's Way

In the 1960s the leadership at Flowers aggressively expanded the company. This accelerated growth, which continues today, was accomplished by acquiring other plants, expanding territory in the southeast and southwest, and building plants with state-of-the-art equipment. In 1968 the real benchmark of industrial success—conversion to public ownership—took place. Initially traded over the counter, the company subsequently moved to the American Stock Exchange and finally to the New York Stock Exchange. In the 1990s Flowers reached the ranks of the Fortune 500 group of corporations.

The remarkable success of what was originally a small town, family-owned bakery was due to many factors, not the least of which was the business acumen and goal setting of the executive leadership.

W.H. Flowers was an amazing man who saw as an independent baker what was happening in the industry—the big guys were gobbling up the smaller ones and to survive you had to get bigger. He was a state senator in the 60s, and I think he wanted to run for governor and would have probably gotten elected. He realized, however, that he had to make a choice either to grow the company or sell it, since it could not remain the size it was. After reaching sales of $18 million in the late 60s, the company became publicly traded.

Another extremely important factor in the success of Flowers was the dedication of the thousands of employees that make up the company. When we talk about success in a company, we're not just thinking about a one-dimensional kind of excellence. We're thinking about various areas lining up. In other words, the accounting department brings their area to excellence, the manufacturing department brings theirs to excellence, and the human resources brings theirs to excellent—all these different departments bringing their areas to excellence indicates a bigger picture of excellence than is seen on the surface. When you think of excellence you normally think of a company that is known for a quality product. But each component of a company must bring excellence to all that they do.

Team Excellence

It's like a football team. Each individual player, whether he is a guard, tackle, center, end, running back, quarterback, defensive linebacker, whatever, brings his position to a level of excellence. And if he was the only one on the team, he would get beat every time. If you had all left guards on the team, you wouldn't win many ball games. But as each one, in their sphere of responsibility, pursues excellence, and the coach teaches them to work together as a team, an awesome football team is birthed.

And that's one of the keys of great coaches. For example, Joe Gibbs of the Washington Redskins is a very successful coach. He went in the car racing business and was very successful in NASCAR because he understood the principle of every person producing excellence without any prima donnas trying to take over. The employees need to see that they are part of something much bigger than themselves. A few years ago, the Yankees had many high-powered players, but they didn't win the American League championship because those players never became part of a well-oiled team.

A friend of mine played football for former Alabama coach Bear Bryant. When I asked him why Coach Bryant was so successful, my friend didn't hesitate with his answer. He said the coach had the ability to take an individual and maximize his talents and skills. This individual then became part of a team with each player contributing maximum efficiency. They were able to depend on one another and function as an efficient unit. W.H. Flowers had this same ability.

How do you get that 100% from everybody? Regardless of the job that people have it is the responsibility of their immediate supervisor to help train and encourage them reach their full potential.

Sometimes people reach the highest position that they can reasonably attain, and there's nothing wrong with that. Although they remain at that position and are content, they can still learn better ways of doing their job. Even if you sweep the floor, you can learn better ways to do it through finding different brooms, cleaning products, or vacuums.

I think that when you have a great team, each member of the team will strive toward excellence in his or her own sphere of responsibility. For example, the financial people must give management accurate statistical information to run the company. The manufacturing people should be aware of the latest equipment and technologies. The marketing people need to work hard to read the pulse beat of the consumer so that the company knows what the consumer wants—not what the company wants to give them. It takes all these facets of the company working hard in their specific areas to make a great team.

Integrity

Excellence, however, is not just being the best in a particular discipline or area. To me, one of the most important questions is: are we operating in integrity? You may be striving to become the best, but it needs to be underlined with integrity and character. When you have those qualities in place, you're eventually going to be a success. Life just works that way.

We bought a lot of bakeries over the years, and invariably if the top people were without integrity or apathetic, then it was the same throughout the organization. A tree dies from the top, and organizations die from the top. Enron died from the top; Tyco died from the top. If there is integrity and character at the top, you will see a strong and sound company all the way down the line.

We had what we called an open door situation at Flowers where our employees could talk with any of our management people. Every once in a while, I received a letter from an employee, complaining about what one or another of our supervisors had done to him or her. Nine out of 10 of the allegations were unfounded, but every one of them was investigated. (I didn't do it personally, but we had somebody that took care of these situations.) If you have an organization composed of people of integrity who work as part of a team, the problems can be resolved easily enough because the people have developed a healthy working relationship with one other.

In some of our acquisitions, we obtained some very good people. It was a challenge, however, to mold their people in with our people. We had some difficult situations to deal with. We couldn't sweep these types of situations under the rug, but we had to deal with them from the outset.

One time, for example, a fellow who had been in the company for a long time was put under someone who had just entered the company through an acquisition. I had known the fellow a long time and I personally went to him, sat down, and talked with him directly about it. He didn't like it, but he made it work; and as he made it work, he began to recognize that the new guy really did have something on the ball.

The important thing is not to let potential problems fester but to deal with them as soon as possible. If you have the lines of communication working well, and you recognize people's gifts and talents, you are going to be able to make the correct decisions and be able to deal with the consequences. Dealing with employees is not rocket science. Having a healthy attitude between both the employees and managers makes all the difference.

Managers also need to recognize who the people are that are going to get on a fast track, so to speak, and progress quickly within the company. Let's say that you had a route salesman who was working for a particular supervisor. This route salesman was effectively producing, so he was quickly moved up to being a supervisor himself, and then to the next level. One day he could very well become the boss of the person he had earlier worked for because he has excelled in his position. His gifts, callings, and talents, along with his maturity, helped him to excel. However, you can't take a 20-year-old, even though he is multi-talented, and put him in charge of an entire company before he has had some years of experience behind him. As you walk through the beginning years of experience, you grow and mature. It is the same thing in Christianity and the whole area of faith. Other people's faith will help you and comfort you, but it's not going to carry you through a crisis. You have to have your own faith.

Management needs to recognize excellence in people, and promote and reward them. When we had our general managers' meetings once a year, I encouraged them to bring their spouses, and we'd have three or four days of meetings. During this time we'd meet half a day and then do other recreational things together, such as golf, the rest of the day. But the purpose of the time was to acknowledge what these managers were doing and let them know we appreciated them. We told them, "Bring your spouse, and let's really enjoy our time together." It's amazing the number of people that would tell me how much that meant to them.

Training

Training employees is such a vital part of developing people. It's great when the company provides these means of increasing the skills and talents of people. (When they don't or when you have a small business yourself, it's imperative that you use self-discipline and find the courses and seminars you need to advance in your profession.) For example, if you have an employee that is an outstanding computer person, but he doesn't work well with people, he either needs to stay right where he is or you need to help him develop skills in dealing with other people.

We continually sent our people to school, as far as upgrading their knowledge and skills, particularly for computers skills and high tech knowledge. In the baking industry, there were new ingredients that would come along, miracle ingredients we called them, that our bakers would need to become familiar with. The baking industry has an American Institute of Bakers in Kansas where Flowers has sent men and women to train for a year. We were constantly encouraging our people to improve their skills and increase their level of knowledge in the industry.

As changes are made throughout the company, the team members need to learn how to effectively and efficiently adopt them. If people don't want to learn more, they are the one talent people. But many times, you will find that the person whom you think is a one talent guy will become a ten talent person because he seizes the opportunities given to him.

The training that people need depends on who they are and what their job is. We didn't send our best salesmen out for classes on baking because that would have driven them up a wall. We sent our salesmen to places where they learned how to better deal with people and connect with them. They needed to know all they could about effective selling for our world today.

The American Management Association was a tremendous resource for training. We also had people in our plants who became trainers of some of the programs. They would take a course on communication, for example, and then return to teach it to our people.

Once we had a young attorney working for us who realized that he needed some more courses in finance, so he took night college courses. I have found that whatever the need is, there is somebody out there that offers a course to help in the training and teaching of employees.

In whatever ways are appropriate, we need to encourage, train, and recognize others' gifts and talents. I think encouragement is so important because it is so easy to get down on yourself. For example, at Flowers if a position became vacant to run a plant, we usually promoted somebody from within the company. Sometimes there were three or four people that would have liked to take the new opening. I used to make it a habit of sitting down and talking to the ones that didn't get the promotion, saying, "Your time is coming, let's see what we can do to help you get to that place where you are ready for new challenges."

Possible Demands

We need to make possible demands on our employees, not impossible ones that frustrate them because they are unattainable. Let's say you have a plant being run by a young plant president that is losing money. You could tell him that within six months you want the plant to be making X amount of money and then let him figure out how to do it, all along knowing there is no way he could ever pull that feat off in six months. You are quite sure that it might take one, two, or even three years to do so. What you've done is put that manager in bondage because of the impossible demand. He may not have good enough equipment, or he's trying to build a good team from the ground up, or he doesn't have the market share yet that could produce the target goal.

It's like the story of the fellow that was given the job to drain the Okee Nokee Swamp. His boss called and told him that he was really running behind schedule and demanded to know what the problem was. The fellow answered him, "Well, when you are up to your neck in alligators, you forget the long-term objective." In other words, you need to give the young plant president the tools and the plausible time schedule in which to make the changes. You need to sit down with him, along with a team of people that understand manufacturing, marketing, plants, productivity, efficiency, and put together a good comprehensive plan on what he needs to do. You then proceed to lay it out—step one, step two, step three, step four—to determine how long it will take to accomplish the goal. We need to give someone a helping hand, rather than demand the impossible from them.

On the other hand, if you had a manufacturing plant in one city, for example, and you bought a bakery in another city but the one in the first was tremendously more efficient than the one in second, you have a decision to make. You could take the production from the one plant and put it in the more efficient plant and make the product for half of what it would have cost you to make it in the closed plant. That's just a good business decision to make.

But then the question is, how do you, as an ethical business person, justify closing the bakery and putting people out of work? It's a very difficult thing to do. But if you have 1,000 total employees, and you close a bakery that has 100 employees in it, what you are doing is leaving the jobs for the 900. The only way to stay in the manufacturing business is with efficiency. There were times when we had to close bakeries because there was no way we could make them as efficient as some of the others. However, we were able to move a lot of people in plants we closed to another one of our plants.

Performance is not a word that is used too often in the Bible, but people have to produce. The word the Bible uses more often is fruit. You have to produce fruit as you work in any organization. You need to recognize your strengths and your weaknesses and see what you can do to increase your strengths. Managers must do the same thing with their employees. It's just a matter of helping the individual improve their knowledge and skills. Continuing education needs to become a way of life, a constant thing that you have to pursue if you want to improve and grow.

CHAPTER FIVE

Dealing With Temptations

There is tremendous pressure on publicly held companies to beat the quarterly projections for sales and profits. I was extremely fortunate to be part of a management team, including the chairman of the board, that never considered questionable accounting practices or other actions to improve the company's financial picture.

From a purely corporate world perspective, we fail when we fall short of reaching our sales and financial objectives. However, God sees a much bigger world and His economy is different, both in terms of objectives and the process of meeting them. As Christians, we go into the journey knowing we will never reach our ultimate goal in this life—to become completely like Christ. It's the lifetime journey itself that matters. Being a Christian in the corporate world means one must take God's view of what constitutes success and submit ourselves to His timetable.

Potential Dangers

I was particularly taken with a speech given by Pat Sajak, host of T.V.'s Wheel of Fortune, at the 2002 Spring Convocation at Hillsdale College in Michigan. He noted that one of the dangers of his business is that it has the potential to fill you with a distorted view of life and of your own importance. It's understandable because people treat you very well. "They send limos for you. They tiptoe around you. They pretend that the most outlandish or inane things you might say are important and quotable. The self-importance that show business can bestow on you seems rather silly to me," he said.

Sajak noted the disconnect between the realities of the people and the perceived realities of many in the entertainment community. I believe that there's not much difference between show business and regular business in this regard. As former CBS newsman Bernard Goldberg wrote in his best-selling book, *Bias*, folks who travel in the same circles, go to the same parties, talk to the same people and compare their ideas to those of like-minded people suffer from social, intellectual, educational and professional inbreeding that creates a sameness of world view. We tend to think that we are the center of the universe, and we have a lock on the truth. What else can explain the decisions made by some of corporate America's top executives? What else could possibly convince the top brass at these powerhouse companies that "cooking the books" is not only acceptable, but a standard business practice? This warped value system could explain why well over half of the top CEOs in America have been on the job for three years or less.

Is it any surprise, then, that a study of 12,474 high school students, released in October 2002 by the Josephson Institute of Ethics, found that 43 percent of all respondents and 41 percent of those bound for college agreed with the following statement: A person has to lie or cheat sometimes in order to succeed. Ten years ago, 34 percent agreed.

Reporter Timothy Lamer argued in an article published last year in *World* magazine that the wave of corporate fraud did not emerge in a vacuum. His view is that it is, in part, a consequence of a society that refuses to recognize absolute standards of right and wrong. This acceptance of situational ethics—what is wrong in one situation may be justifiable in another—is the ultimate exercise of rationalization. Former Wal-Mart COO Don Soderquist, founder of the Soderquist Center for Leadership and Ethics in Siloam Springs, Arkansas, told Lamer that most books on business ethics mistakenly focus on behavior. That misses the mark, he said. "It's not what you do, but what you believe. Behavior will always be governed by what you believe."

Ethics

"Ethics" comes from the Greek word meaning character. Christian ethics measures the greatest good and the highest morality, which can only come from following the will of God as it is revealed in the Bible.

I talk a pretty good game when it comes to ethics, but it hasn't been that long since God showed me a few chinks in my own armor. I love to hunt and I really enjoy shooting doves. In Georgia, it's common practice to bait doves (putting feed out to attract birds to your hunting site). It doesn't seem to matter much that it's illegal. And so it was that New Year's Day 2001 found me in the back woods of Pavo shooting doves—baited doves. Given the fact that I was out in the middle of nowhere, I was surprised when two game wardens, one from the feds and one from the state, walked up. *How did these guys get here?* I wondered. But I knew even before I completed the thought that God had sent them. He wasn't going to allow me to stand on a soapbox and talk about ethics and the Kingdom of God when I was walking around doing things I knew I should not be doing. Suffice it to say, I don't bait doves any more.

There's no question in my mind that my conduct was sending a terrible message to my children and my grandchildren: It's okay for Christians to bend the rules so that they can have a little fun as long as they're not doing anything really bad. We can have our cake and eat it too. But that's not how it works. How we make our small decisions reflects on how we'll make the big decisions.

We get in real trouble when we start justifying our conduct and try to differentiate a minor offense from a major one. Does it really matter whether we cheat a little or a lot? One of my favorite people, President Ronald Reagan, answered the question this way:

> The character that takes command in moments
> of crucial choices has already been determined
> by a thousand other choices made earlier in
> seemingly unimportant moments.

When we are in a position of authority, we have a tremendous responsibility, both at home and in the workplace to do the right thing—always. We can't fudge things. If the top button of an overcoat isn't buttoned right, all the buttons below will be misaligned. It works the same way with a family or a corporation: What's going on at the top is reflected in the actions of those at every level of the organization.

The Ten Commandments don't allow much wiggle room. It's not a menu that you can pick and choose from. They don't proclaim, "Do not kill him unless...," or "Do not steal if...." I'm reminded of the little boy who broke a window in his home with a baseball. When his mother confronted him and his friends, nobody confessed. "You know," said the mom, "Honesty is the best policy." The little boy looked askance and asked, "What's the second best?" I know that God has endless patience for His children, but it must be sorely tested when we engage in situational ethics.

Regardless of our station in life, when we are— or think we are—important, we inevitably will face four major stumbling blocks. Any one of them—ego, lust, greed or a spirit of unforgiveness—can bring us down, whether we are entry level workers, middle managers, or CEOs. It's the same, no matter where we are in our careers. It's not a matter of if we'll fail, but only when. Many in corporate America, unfortunately, have been consumed by one of these stumbling blocks. And while there are many good people in boardrooms and executive suites across the country, none of us is immune.

Ego

USA Today in 2002 reported the results of a Roper poll of the wealthiest one percent of American families—those with incomes of at least $250,000 and/or net worth of at least $2.5 million. They were asked what they would pay for different opportunities. The average they'd shell out for being president was $55,000. They said they'd spend $407,000 for great intellect and $487,000 for true love. The value they put on a place in heaven was $640,000. The very idea that anyone thinks they can buy their way into heaven with a suitcase of dollar bills is ludicrous. But the fact that they have at least $2.5 million and are willing to spend less than a quarter of it on eternal life makes you wonder what they think they're going to do with the rest of the money. The ultimate irony is that access to heaven is absolutely free!

I know firsthand what it's like to be on a power trip. I had a lot of power at a fairly early age with many people's jobs depending on me. I sensed that I might be a little bit better than the next guy because I was calling the shots. At work, I once had the reputation of being a tough taskmaster. During that time many of my subordinates responded to me out of fear rather than out of loyalty or respect. Thank God He helped me see my error before I had gotten too far. As I've said, I think it is extremely difficult for anyone in a position of power in the corporate world to be humble. Our arrogance can get the best of us. I've seen people take advantage of their authority, using subordinates as a whipping post. The same thing happens at home, where we expect everything to revolve around us just because we're there. A number of the nation's former top executives are looking for new employment and/or new spouses precisely because they let their egos run wild.

Several years ago, I saw an example of ego in the making in a young executive at Flowers Foods. We had a corporate jet that ferried the executive team between corporate headquarters and our plants. This fellow, I'll call him John, was running late getting to the airport and knew that the plane and all aboard were waiting for him. But it wasn't a big deal, he reasoned, since he'd checked the passenger manifest and saw he outranked the others. What John didn't know was that a crisis had developed at one of the plants that required my personal attention. I was one of those waiting.

When he spotted me as he boarded the plane, a look of sheer terror crossed John's face. "I wouldn't have been late if I'd known you'd be on the plane," he confided anxiously. "I didn't know you were flying."

I didn't say anything in front of the others, but the first chance I had, I called John into my office. It didn't take long for me to convince him that he needed to show more respect for his co-workers, whether they were below him on the corporate ladder or above him. That young man is now a key leader with Flowers Foods.

Jesus Christ was a real, living, breathing man, the Son of God. With His ability to heal the sick, the lame and the blind, to cast out demons and to raise the dead—not to mention the fact that his Father was creator and CEO of the universe—you might think that Jesus would have developed an ego. He was obviously a success. Instead of traveling across the Holy Land, He could have made the masses come to Him. Instead of going to the cross for our sins, He could have said, "I don't need this. You made your own bed. Now lie in it." But He didn't.

How does a person advance in the business world and not become a power seeker? It has to do with our attitude and our priorities. There is a significant difference between recognizing and cultivating our gifts and attempting to build a power base for our own ego. The power that we receive from God is to be used for His purposes.

Lust

Unfortunately, when we think of lust nowadays, we're just as likely to think of a fallen priest or other members of the clergy as we are to think of a Hollywood celebrity. So many business leaders, politicians and others in the public eye have fallen to temptation that it's just not news anymore. We've seen men and women succumb to temptation who had everything you could want in the world. And if they didn't have it, someone could get it for them. They had intelligence, money, good looks, charm, political savvy, and wives who stood by them even when the chips were down. They were powerful figures, some of them held up as the titans of the corporate or political realm. What more could any person want? But they stumbled over lust.

Some people enjoy the knowledge that they can have anything that they desire. Each conquest temporarily satisfies their lust and boosts their self-esteem. If I'm in it for a quick fix, lust is for me, but there's no long-term satisfaction in it. There's no stopping point. We can't win. Just as death and destruction are never satisfied, so human desire is never satisfied.

Lust is nothing new. It's not a phenomenon of the industrial age. Lust was rampant in the Old Testament. Samson lusted after Delilah, ultimately losing all his power to obtain her.

In the last several years, I've had several men tell me they were hooked on pornography and needed help. I think pornography is one of the most rampant things that Satan is using right now in the body of Christ. It's straight from the pit. As Jack Hayford says, you're two clicks away from it. I personally have a filter on my computer. My local internet server has it and when the installer put it on, he asked if I wanted the code to break the filter. I refused to have the code because I don't want anything to do with what it filters out.

People who want to be free from their involvement with pornography need to realize that it's like having a piece of machinery in need of repair. When it's opened, the filth inside is revealed. After you clean out the filth, you need to do preventative maintenance, which is so often what people forget to do. Once you are free from something like pornography, you need to take positive steps, such as prayer, to prevent it from happening again. To overcome something like this, a person has to recognize the problem and then have in place a set of values that causes them to not only take care of it but also maintain their freedom from it.

Men and women in business have to recognize that they are going to be tempted in today's world. But when they are tempted, the question is whether or not they have the backbone, the value system, and the love of the Lord to walk away from it. Joseph is a perfect example. Potiphar's wife lusted after Joseph, but Joseph turned her down. The Bible says Joseph ran, he just didn't take a little casual walk outside, he ran away from the advances of Potipher's wife.

David, on the other hand, didn't run from it. David lusted after Bathsheba and she became his lover. When she became pregnant with David's child, he sent her husband out to the front lines of the battlefield where he faced a certain death. Here's a man after God's own heart that loved the Lord, wrote most of the Psalms, yet he fell into temptation. So it's not something any of us can ignore. We must have the shield of faith around us for protection at all times.

But lust isn't limited to sexual conduct. We can lust after the gamut of material things. In the New Testament, John writes of "lust for physical pleasure, the lust for everything we see, and pride in our possessions. These are not from the Father. They are from this evil world. And this world is fading away, along with everything it craves" (1 John 2:16-17).

Ecclesiastes, in the Old Testament, includes this commentary:

> *I tried to find meaning by building huge homes for myself and planting beautiful vineyards...I collected great sums of silver and gold...I had everything a man could desire. But as I looked at everything I had worked so hard to accomplish, it was all so meaningless. It was like chasing the wind. There was nothing really worthwhile anywhere* (Eccl. 2:4,8,11).

As human beings, we always want more. Jacqueline and I have a beautiful condo on the Gulf of Mexico. Over the last few years, development in the area has been phenomenal. When I'm walking on the beach, I often catch myself thinking about how nice it would be to have a bigger, nicer condo. "If only I had bought more property five years ago," I chide myself, "I'd have it made." But on a deeper level, I know that's not something I should be concerned about. As I Timothy 6:6 tells us, "Godliness with contentment is great gain" (NIV).

Lust almost always involves desiring something we shouldn't. People with a godly value system don't invite temptation. We must not place ourselves in compromising situations, not because we're better than anybody else, but because we are just like everybody else. The fact is that powerful people often want it ALL. Yet when they get what they think is the final piece of the puzzle, they find that something still is missing.

The only way to get it ALL is to be willing to GIVE IT ALL UP to walk with God. To do this we first have to realize that it all came from God to begin with, and we are only temporary stewards of it during our time here on earth. Therefore, we really are not giving up anything since it belongs to Him. When we come to this realization, we have made a major step forward in our maturing as a Christian.

Greed

The Old Testament book of Proverbs is a profoundly practical look at the consequences of our human foibles. King Solomon, who wrote much of the book, had a few things to say about greed.

Choose a good reputation over great riches, for being held in high esteem is better than having silver or gold (Prov. 22:1).

A greedy person tries to get rich quick, but it only leads to poverty. Greed causes fighting; trusting the Lord leads to prosperity (Prov. 28:22,25).

Not a day passes that newspaper headlines don't remind us how greed is alive and well in corporate America. Insider trading seems to be pervasive. It is, perhaps, an unintended result of attempts to tie the performance of top executives to compensation that often took the form of stock options. When there is a direct relationship between your personal finances and the company's bottom line, there's a powerful incentive to take shortcuts or to outright cheat. The problem isn't the options and business incentives themselves. The problem is greed. The parade of corporate executives before Congress and the courts is a sad affair.

Ask yourself this question: If you owned 500,000 shares of your company's stock valued at

$94 per share, and you knew because of your position in the organization that the value was going to plummet within a matter of days, would you be tempted to dump it even though you knew that the trade would be illegal? The answer almost certainly is a resounding, "Yes!" We are tempted every day of our lives. But would you do it, knowing that it was illegal? That's the acid test. Acid cuts to the very core. Who are you? Are you one person when you know someone's watching and another when you're in the room alone? As Christians in the marketplace, we have to pass the acid test every day because we are operating in a place where our decision making can compromise our values. And because so much of what we do involves money—the bottom line—we are particularly vulnerable to greed.

Greed can consume us. If making and keeping money is the focus of our lives, we miss out on countless opportunities. We cheat ourselves and, too often, we end up hurting others. Just think of the tens of thousands of workers who have lost their jobs and most or all of their retirement funds in the wake of the latest corporate scandals. Think of the shareholders who have been left in the lurch.

Several years ago I bought some silver options and made a killing. Well, not a killing, but decent money. I told the guy that I was dealing with, "I'm going to take my seed money and let's get back into this thing. Let's get some more." And in a matter of four or five weeks, it was all gone. The market does these type of things. And God gently said to me, "You really ran into a greed problem here. You took your seed money out. Why didn't you turn around and take that money that you made and sow it into the kingdom of God?"

What about the former CEO who allegedly sold off more than $10 million in company stock in the 48 hours immediately preceding the announcement that a promising drug developed by his company would not be approved by the FDA? Meanwhile the average investor got stuck with a stock that has lost more than 90% of its value since the FDA decision was made public. I've been there, myself. At one time, I had stock options in Flowers Foods. The stock was selling at a then all-time high of $27 per share. Because of my position at the company, I knew the value of that stock was going to fall quite a bit. But legally I couldn't do anything about it. When I finally was able to exercise my options, the price had dropped considerably. At a different time in my life, before I got my priorities in order, I might not have taken the high road. Did I like losing out on all that money? No way. But I did like being able to look at myself in the mirror the next morning, knowing that I had made the right decision.

More than 2,000 years ago, the apostle Paul wrote to Timothy, a young man at the time, about the dangers inherent in greed.

People who long to be rich fall into temptation and are trapped by many foolish and harmful desires that plunge them into ruin and destruction. For the love of money is at the root of all kinds of evil. And some people, craving money, have wandered from the faith and pierced themselves with many sorrows (1 Tim. 6:9-10).

Paul goes on to tell Timothy that he should tell those who are rich in this world not to be proud and not to trust in their money.

Tell them to use their money to do good. They should be rich in good works and should give generously to those in need, always being ready to share with others what God has given them (1 Tim. 6:18).

We all are personally acquainted with greed. In my case, it reared its ugly head just before I retired from Flowers Foods. When I told the chairman of the board that I was planning to retire—I like to call it refocusing—he asked me what I wanted in the way of a retirement package. I laid out a half dozen things that I thought were reasonable, and he said, "No problem. I'll take it to the executive committee." The first thought that came into my mind when he so readily agreed to my proposal was, "I didn't ask for enough." That was a thought that I had to quickly refuse to consider. Our flesh is weak, but we must overcome it with the grace God gives us.

After I began my journey with God, I started to give my tithe (10%). Of course, I wasn't making much money at the time, so the checks weren't very big. But as my career advanced and I began to make more money, tithing got harder. I discovered that it's much easier to write a check for $100 than it is to write one for $10,000. But it's not just about tithing; it's about being a cheerful giver in the broadest possible sense of the word.

In the New Testament, Paul writes that the farmer who plants only a few seeds will get a small crop. "But the one who plants generously will get a generous crop. You must each make up your own mind as to how much you should give. Don't give reluctantly or in response to pressure. For God loves the person who gives cheerfully. And God will generously provide all that you need" (2 Cor. 9:6-8).

The fact that the time of reaping isn't always on our timetable tests our faithfulness. In sowing and reaping, the reaping so often comes years later. At my farm in Pavo, it may be 12 to 15 years from the time I planted my pine seedlings to the point when I start to realize a return on my investment.

I am learning to become a cheerful giver and a good steward of what the Lord has entrusted me with. I can honestly say that it's no longer painful for me to write out a check to the church or a needy organization or individual. In fact, over and over God has proven Himself faithful to me and blessed me beyond my wildest dreams when I trust Him in my giving. The average American gives only about two percent of his or her income to the church and all charities combined. If only people would discover that God can be trusted with our material needs just like every other part of our life.

In Proverbs, Solomon tells us that we are to honor the Lord with our wealth. "Then He will fill your barns with grain and your vats will overflow with the finest wine" (Prov. 3:10). In Ecclesiastes, he really hits the nail on the head. "Those who love money will never have enough" (Eccl. 5:10). (More will be discussed about finances in Chapter 8.)

Unforgiveness

Another stumbling block we come up against is unforgiveness. It's almost impossible to enjoy the game if you spend all of your time keeping score. I used to keep score. It was very difficult for me to forgive people, even if their offense was un-intentional. While I didn't keep a "hit list" in my billfold, like one fellow I know, I carried around a lot of bitterness. It can eat you alive. It gets to the point where the bitterness is no longer focused on an individual or situation; it invades every corner of your life and warps your thinking.

Unforgiveness is rampant in business. You have to constantly watch your back. The problem is that while you're looking back, you can't move forward.

If anyone ever had a right to be bitter, it was Joseph, whose story is told in Genesis. Joseph was his father's favorite. Being the youngest, he seemed to delight in telling on his brothers when they did something that Jacob, their father, wouldn't approve of. Like any pesky little brother might do, Joseph tormented them with his dreams, which always seemed to show Joseph in a more favorable light. Because he was such a good son, Jacob gave Joseph a special gift, a beautiful robe of many colors. Joseph's brothers hated him.

One day, Jacob sent Joseph out to check on his brothers' shepherding. When they saw him approaching in the distance, they hatched a plan to kill him. But before they could carry out the plan, one of the brothers persuaded the others to spare his life and sell him to slave traders instead. When they returned home without Joseph, they convinced their father that he had been killed by wild animals.

Joseph spent the next 13 years as a slave in Egypt. Ultimately, he became the king's most trusted servant, the second most powerful man in Egypt. When he finally had the opportunity to avenge his betrayal at his brothers' hands, Joseph, instead, embraced them. "Don't be afraid of me. Am I God to judge and punish you? As far as I am concerned, God turned into good what you meant for evil" (Gen. 50:19-20).

There aren't many Josephs among us. When we walk in unforgiveness, it undermines our motivation and keeps us from doing God's work. If Joseph had been preoccupied with getting back at his brothers, he wouldn't have been able to carry out what God had called him to do. The entire course of history might have been different.

I'm not a social worker. If an employee still couldn't or wouldn't do the job after much counseling, training and other assistance, they had to leave the company. You must have good people working for you, and you must be able to count on them to do their jobs. There always will be people who will try to take advantage of you if they think you are vulnerable. In fact, some folks think Christians are a bunch of weaklings because we turn the other cheek. But forgiveness shouldn't be mistaken for stupidity or naiveté. If we follow Jesus' advice, we'll be "wise as serpents, but harmless as doves" (Matt. 10:16 NKJ).

Ego, lust, greed and unforgiveness are formidable stumbling blocks because they are so much an innate part of the human nature. If we let them take over our lives, we can lose our jobs and our families. But most importantly, we can fritter away our opportunity to be the people that God intended us to be.

CHAPTER SIX

Business as a Ministry

Being a Christian in the marketplace is a full-time ministry. It's every bit as important as the work that a paid pastor or member of a church staff will do. Who we are in our Christian walk has a tremendous effect on the people around us.

The most significant aspect of our marketplace ministry is that it happens in the real world wherein lie the real temptations that we discussed in the previous chapter. How we respond to those temptations and challenges is very important. We are being watched. The best sermon we can preach is the one we walk.

The cornerstone of Christian leadership is that we can't expect the people we're leading to be what we are not. We have to lead by example. In a letter to Timothy, Paul admonishes him to be an example to all believers "in what you teach, in the way you live, in your love, your faith and your purity" (1 Tim. 4:12). Jesus didn't spend all His time in the synagogues lecturing on how Jews should live their lives. He spent most off His time out in the real world of His day, not talking, but doing.

In fact, Jesus took the religious leaders of His day to task. He cautioned His followers to practice and obey whatever the Pharisees said to them, but not to follow their example.

> *For they do not practice what they teach. They crush you with impossible demands and never lift a finger to help ease the burden. Everything they do is for show* (Matt. 23:3-5).

As Christians in the marketplace, we are called to be overcomers. Overcomers are bold; they have grace and power; they hear His voice; they are people of faith. If we are to be overcomers, we must be able to look beyond the obvious—to peel away the veneer—and uncover the motives that drive the day's events. We must be people of patience and perseverance. Overcomers are called to put God's desires above their own.

In the marketplace, our resolve will be tested at every turn, and because we are human, we will sometimes stumble. We are up against the giants of the 21st century: unbelief in God; a "live-and-let-live" mentality, which holds no one accountable to a universally accepted standard of conduct (situational ethics); the uncertainty of our economy; the cumulative effects of dishonesty and greed in corporate America; and the disconnect between reality and the perceptions of many of our business leaders. If we're not ready for these challenges, we will fall.

Jesus provided a blueprint for leadership. He challenged the Sadducees, the teachers of the religious law, and the Pharisees, the official interpreters of the scriptures, whom He viewed as hypocrites. He revealed His warrior mentality. This is not the gentle Jesus with the little children at His feet!

In no uncertain terms, Jesus identified six qualities that set apart true leaders in Matthew 23:3-5.

1. Leaders do not appoint themselves.

2. Leaders practice what they preach.

3. Leaders do not hold their followers in bondage, making impossible demands and never offering a helping hand.

4. Leaders care about the needs of others.

5. Leaders do not revel in the glory of their power and position.

6. Leaders are more concerned with their ability to serve others than they are with their titles.

Jesus' message describing leadership is just as applicable to us today as it was 2,000 years ago. I believe that true leadership is developed and sustained by vision. Our vision is a direct reflection of our values, which are shaped by our desire to live according to God's will for our lives. A leader who lacks vision will never reach his or her full potential in any aspect of life.

I've been asked why I think so many leaders in the business world have found themselves being shown the door. There are the usual reasons for failure cited in any management book: not wanting the goal or vision badly enough; or on the other hand, wanting the goal or vision too badly; failing to communicate and relate effectively with others; and failing to recognize and use others' strengths and resources. For some it is a matter of ethics. But the bottom line is that we take the first steps down the road to failure the moment we begin to walk outside God's will for our lives.

Whenever we get the chance, Jacqueline and I spend time at the beach with our children and grandchildren. One day we spent several hours with my then 18-month-old granddaughter, Ashley, building sandcastles. As soon as we had completed work on one of our sandcastles, Ashley would knock it down. She delighted in the total devastation of our handiwork.

As sunset approached, we had little to show for our efforts. But just down the beach, about 15 yards from our construction site, another family had built one of the most impressive sandcastles I've ever seen. It had turrets and flags and elaborate artwork decorating the walls. It was a masterpiece. I could tell that Ashley was just itching to knock it down, but she knew its creators had intended it to stay for the duration of the weekend.

Her dad—my son Howard—and I kept an eye on her as she edged away from us toward the sandcastle. When she was about halfway there, Howard told her to turn around and come back to us. This ran counter to her plans. She crossed her little arms in front of her and thrust her chest out in defiance. She stood there pouting, contemplating her next move. Her gaze shifted back and forth between Howard and the sandcastle. "Dad," Howard said, "You're seeing a vivid example of someone dealing with a choice between good and evil."

In the end, Ashley overcame temptation and walked back toward us. The reason she did it was out of obedience to her father. She had no clue how much her dad loved her in trying to teach her a lesson in restraint. That is so apropos for hard-charging people that are consistently faced with making decisions between good and evil.

At the risk of sounding simplistic, I'm a firm believer that what sets apart the Christian leader from the rest of the pack is the ability to discern the difference between good and evil. The decisions of all the big guys at the Tycos, Enrons and World Coms basically involved a choice between right and wrong, good and evil. If just one person in a leadership role had asked, "What's the right thing to do?" things might have turned out very differently.

There's no question that when a company is losing money there is tremendous pressure to turn things around. It's often easier to take short cuts than it is to do the right thing. And when ego kicks in, it's easy to convince yourself that you are above being caught.

When I was at Flowers Foods, the baking industry was a small fraternity of people who knew everybody in it. It would have been very easy to justify having a friendly talk with a competitor about pricing. But that's called price fixing, and in my book, not only would it have been illegal, it would have been wrong.

I think it's a given in most any organization that, if you want to get ahead, you find out what pleases your boss. As Christians in the marketplace, it is absolutely critical that we know with a certainty what pleases the Lord. The Bible tells us that all He asks of us is obedience.

In the corporate world, once we cross the line between right and wrong, it's next to impossible to steer ourselves back in the right direction. In the case of the recent corporate failures, when things began to fall apart, it was like pulling a loose bit of yarn on a sweater. The whole thing quickly unraveled.

Business executives face constant pressure to perform. It's unbelievable. At Flowers Foods, I had to deliver profit and loss statements every week. And as a publicly held company, we had to report our earnings every quarter. There's no question that how I dealt with that pressure affected the people who worked for me.

W.H. Flowers had an uncanny ability to cut to the root of a problem. Any good executive has that ability too. Mr. Flowers also had a knack for pushing you right to the edge to get every ounce out of you. Just before you would fall off the cliff, he would pull you back.

Most corporate executives will tell you that union negotiations are extraordinarily high pressured. When you reach an impasse and a strike is called, everybody loses. One of our managers had successfully dealt with some very serious labor problems related to acquisitions in Houston, Baton Rouge, and Miami. He was our point man or field colonel in taking the hill. What none of us realized until it was nearly too late was that he was close to the breaking point, and as a result of the pressure cooker environment he worked in, he had developed a substance abuse problem.

Had he been in the military, this manager would have been awarded the Congressional Medal of Honor. But in the corporate world, he now was viewed as a liability. I was under tremendous pressure to give him early retirement. Had I done so, that pressure immediately would have dissipated. But I was quite certain that he had many more productive years ahead of him and refused to release him. Instead, I took him off the front lines and got him into rehab. Because I was faithful to Him, God took care of me and smoothed the ruffled feathers at work, and the manager later returned and continued to contribute to the success of the company.

To some, my refusal to give early retirement to this manager may seem like a bold action. But more often than not, it's the small things that set apart the Christian leader. So many books are written on the extraordinary that we tend to overlook the ordinary.

We had a fellow on the corporate staff whose wife was expecting a baby any day. I flew out of town to one of our plants and was shocked when I saw him there. "What in the world are you doing here?" I asked. "Why aren't you at home where you belong?" He was flabbergasted. In his attempt to be loyal to the company and to excel at his job, it had never occurred to him that someone in management might think he had his priorities out of order. Some time later, he stopped me in the hallway and reminded me of the incident. He had gotten home just in time for the birth of his daughter. "You'll never know how much that meant to me," he said.

A number of companies are urging their workers to put God first, family second, and work third. I think that's a bold action. Chick-Fil-A is closed on Sundays. I think that's pretty bold. But the ultimate act of boldness is when we walk as a Christian in the marketplace and refuse to compromise our values.

Power of Prayer

Never underestimate the power of prayer in the marketplace. It's phenomenal! In union negotiations, there are Christians on both sides of the table. You have to pray for wisdom. In Romans, we are reassured that "God causes everything to work together for the good of those who love Him and are called according to His purpose for them" (Rom. 8:28).

In marketplace ministry, we know we are doing the right thing when the peace of God is with us. Once you've experienced it, it's clear that there's no other way to live. In a letter to the Colossians, the apostle Paul urged them to "let the peace that comes from Christ rule in your hearts.

Work hard and cheerfully at whatever you do, as though you were working for the Lord rather than for people. Remember that the Lord will give you an inheritance as your reward, and the master you are serving is Christ. But if you do what is wrong, you will be paid back for the wrong that you have done (Col. 3:23-25).

As I look back over my career, my greatest regret is that I didn't always fully trust God to be faithful even though He had never given one reason to doubt Him. To be truly effective as a Christian in the marketplace, you have to have absolute trust in God. For most can-do people, that seems like an extraordinarily naive statement. How ironic it is that truly bright people are so often confused by the simple things.

Paul recognized this when he wrote to the people of Corinth during one of his missionary journeys.

I know how foolish the message of the cross sounds to those who are on the road to destruction. But we who are being saved recognize this message as the very power of God. As the Scriptures say, 'I will destroy human wisdom and discard their most brilliant

ideas.' So where does this leave the philoso-
phers, the scholars and the world's brilliant
debaters? God has made them all look foolish
and has shown their wisdom to be useless
nonsense.... This foolish plan of God is far
wiser than the wisest human plans, and God's
weakness is far stronger than the greatest of
human strength (1 Cor. 1:18-20,25).

If we look back over our lives and are truly grateful for all that God has done for us, it's easier to look at the future with faith in what He is going to do. The end result of not trusting God is frustration and confusion.

In corporate America, it's a cutthroat world, but we are not forced to wield the knives. We don't have to storm the executive suite and proclaim our faith. We don't have to turn stockholder meetings into Hallelujah sessions. We don't have to convert everyone in the organization to Christianity. All God asks is that we, as individuals, be faithful to Him all the time.

Godly living is radically different from what most of us see prevalent in society today. It requires a radical change in our speech, conduct and thinking. We don't have to go to Babylon or Egypt. We can accomplish our work on Wall Street or Main Street. It all comes back to how we conduct ourselves. Nothing speaks more powerfully than our actions.

The River Jordan

At some point in our lives all of us are confronted by our own personal River Jordan. In the Bible, the River Jordan stood between the Israelites, who had been wandering in the desert for 40 years, and the Promised Land. As the feet of the priests who were carrying the Ark of the Covenant touched the water, the river stopped flowing and the riverbed dried up, allowing them to safely cross to the other side. The Israelites crossed their River Jordan with dry feet.

Most of us have a River Jordan in our lives. Some of these are self-made. Others are a part of God's plan for our lives. My River Jordan was retirement. I didn't want to leave the business world. I enjoyed it. I liked the salary, the people, and the perks. Retirement wasn't on my timetable. But God was telling me, "It's time to leave. I've got something else for you to do." It was on His timetable. Pride nearly kept me from crossing the river, but humility won out.

Obedience to God offers an unbelievable return on investment. It protects us from evil. It helps us keep a clear conscience. It brings peace in our lives. Obedience is not bondage. When God tells us to cross the river, we can be certain that it's the right thing to do. And He will give us the means to cross it. It may require a paradigm shift in the way we think and the way we go about doing things, but obedience brings great rewards.

Not long ago, Jacqueline and I were in Atlanta, staying on the 10th floor of a hotel. In the morning, I looked out the window and began praying. Our room overlooked chaotic, six-lane Peachtree Street. As I watched, a woman and a little girl approached the corner. The woman held the hand of the little girl, who was dancing with delight. The woman punched the button that signals that a pedestrian is waiting to cross the street. Within a minute, Peachtree traffic from all directions at all nearby intersections had stopped, and the two of them walked right across what, only moments before, had been an untraversable torrent of traffic. God speaks to me in different ways.

That morning He spoke to me through the woman and that little girl. "Heeth," He said, "all I want you to do is to hold My hand." If that little girl had gotten to the intersection without her mother, it would have been disastrous. She had absolutely no idea of the danger. And it's like that with us and our River Jordans. We will be able to safely cross the Jordans in our lives if we take His hand and let Him lead the way.

CHAPTER SEVEN

Serving Others

In business, our climb up the corporate ladder defines us. I am a fiercely competitive individual and for many years my mentality was to conquer. But as I began to read the Bible and to study, I saw that's not the way that Jesus did it. I learned not to fear meekness. Meekness is power under control. It is about our willingness to place God above our own egos. Weakness is our refusal to trust God.

We also have to deal with the issue of humility that Jesus talks about so much. It's extremely difficult to be humble in the corporate world. They just don't offer courses in humility in America's business schools. There's a change in our mindset that needs to take place. Instead of viewing others in light of what they can do to help us get from point A to point B, we need to see how we can help others move from their point A to point B.

Perhaps the most poignant example of humility in the Bible is detailed in the book of John, when the disciples gathered to celebrate the Passover meal, known as the Seder, with Jesus. Jesus knew that this would be their last meal together and that Judas would betray him within hours.

Now bear in mind what the streets were like back in those days. There was no pavement. Beasts of burden pulled carts through the streets; animals roamed freely. There was no sanitation system to dispose of human waste. The people walked in the streets shod only in sandals. There were no foot deodorizers. There were no cushioned insoles to prevent blisters and festering sores. Not even for disciples.

Jesus knew that the Father had given Him authority over everything and that He had come from God and would return to God. So He got up from the table, took off his robe, wrapped a towel around his waist, and poured water into a basin. Over their protests, He began to wash the disciples' feet and to wipe them with

*the towel He had around Him. When He had
finished, Jesus told them, "I have given you an
example to follow. Do as I have done to you"*
(John 13:1-5,17).

Can you imagine a modern day CEO calling in
his managers and proceeding to wash their feet?
What Jesus did boggles the mind and defines what
leadership is all about.

Power can do strange things to people. I'll go
out on a limb here and say that there probably
aren't a whole lot of corporate executives who see
themselves as servants, either at work or at home.
I know that, for many years, I wasn't one. But
when I became a Christian, I felt that God had
called me to change, and I tried to start incorporating His value system into every aspect of my
life. It began to dawn on me that I was really there
to serve, not only the board of directors and the
stockholders, but the people who worked for me
as well. And the best way I knew to serve them
was to help them grow in what they were doing.
That meant that I had to add two new words to
my vocabulary: patience and grace.

While I still had my moments, I tried to be pa-
tient when people made mistakes or experienced
failure. Instead of chopping their heads off, l
would ask them why they felt things had not
worked out and how we might work together to
make it right. I tried my best to create an atmos-

phere in which people would enjoy their work and give them a platform for their success. I wanted them to have the opportunity to explore and fully develop their professional talents, gifts and callings. I tried to apply the same principles at home.

For example, I learned quite a bit through one situation when we were trying to find a man with good manufacturing and production skills and experience. We interviewed a lot of different people, finally narrowing it down to about two or three of them. I took one of them out to dinner with my wife, Jacqueline. This guy was good: he understood plans, he understood our baking ingredients and their use in our products. After we returned home that night, Jacqueline said, "There's something about him I didn't like." And I said, "Well, Jacqueline," I said, "You just weren't with it." She said, "I'm just being honest with you; there's something about the man I didn't like." At the time I didn't recognize it, but my wife was using her gift of discernment.

Three months after we hired him, we found that this guy had walked in deception. He didn't have to do it because he had the ability to meet the job requirements, but he was so insecure that he had fabricated some of his degrees and experience. And of course, we had to let him go. But if I had listened to my wife in that situation, we could have avoided the problem. She had good discernment and picked up on something in the man's spirit. She was serving me when she shared what she did. I just didn't accept her service at the time.

How does a business man know when to listen to his wife? I think there needs to be a mutual trust that has to be built between the two of them. I have no question in my mind that my wife hears from God. It's just like selling the vacation condominium we have. We both came to one mind together that we would sell it. Now we don't pray for ten minutes about where we're going to eat, that's not what I'm talking about. But we do spend time in prayer together concerning the big decisions we need to make, such as selling the condo. To do that, husbands have to have a trust factor with their wives and vice versa.

I need to give my wife enough room and enough security so that she feels free to share with me. She never had that until some time after I had become a Christian because I didn't understand how to do it. I eventually learned how to give her the room to be who she is. It's like with the kids—I was such a tough taskmaster, my kids reached the point where they didn't want to talk to me about things that were really bothering them. Before I understood this principle, they only wanted to talk about things that made me feel good but not about their problems.

God showed me that I needed to help my wife

realize that I cherished her and appreciated who she was, and I wasn't trying to make her become somebody else. I let her know that I was willing to listen to her and to hear what she had to say. She began to be open with me when she saw how I didn't put her down when she told me something.

If my wife comes to me and starts sharing something, it's real easy for a person with my personality to start solving her problem before she even gets it out on the table. And that makes her not want to share anything further with me. But I've come a long way, and it reflects on how our relationship with each other has improved. Of course the same thing applies to my wife. I might be sharing something with Jacqueline and she has learned not to preach me a little sermon rather than really listen to what I'm saying. It all boils down to having a trust relationship with one another.

It's the same principle of working with people in business. They won't have a trust relationship with you and share their concerns with you if you're constantly raising your voice or belittling them, or if something goes wrong and you jump on them right away.

Your employees need to be in a position where they don't mind telling you what's going on because they have that trust factor that you're not going to react to them. It's not that you don't correct people. It's all about whether or not you handle problems with grace and wisdom.

Some people just can't handle power. We had people that progressed in the company and began having a lot of people working under them. Unfortunately they never realized that their mission was to serve the people under them.

It took me a while to always remember that I was there to serve both the people that worked under me and the ones that were above me on the corporate ladder.

Cutting Off the Ear

I believe that Peter did not know Jesus' heart when it came to his response to the guard when they came to arrest Jesus. Peter was furious, pulled his sword out, and cut the guard's ear off. Jesus' response? He healed the ear. It is interesting that almost immediately afterwards, Peter denied the Lord three times. There was a certain amount of strong pride in Peter that rose up when Jesus had told him earlier that he would deny Him. And that pride says, "I'm strong; I can handle anything."

Jesus knew that Peter would deny him three times because he had to deal with his issue of pride. Then later Jesus asked him three times if Peter loved him The third time when Peter answered, he said, "Lord, you know all things." He was telling Jesus that his boastfulness and pride were replaced by love. He realized that Jesus did not want him to be a weak but rather strong and without pride. And I believe in my own personal life, my ear cutting was because there was pride in me that hadn't been dealt with. I think that it is typical throughout corporate America. The only way to put away pride and become humble is to increase your love capacity for the Lord.

I had a fellow that had misused some company funds. He and his wife came in to see me, and I immediately verbally "cut both their ears off." I was absolutely wrong in the way I handled that situation. I went back and apologized to both of them. Not that what he did wasn't wrong, but I was wrong in the way I handled it. I went back to him and told him how sorry I was that I had mishandled it. They received it because they saw my sincerity. The man had to leave the company because it was a pretty serious situation, but it was an opportunity for me to have more grace.

I was wrong in the ways I had handled some things in the past with my kids, and I needed to change. My youngest son, who has five kids, was staying at our home for three or four days, and he and I got in a disagreement over a very petty thing and I cut his ear off. And as soon as I did, I realized what I had done. And I guess in one sense I was like Peter. I knew I was wrong and so I apologized to him. It was amazing what it did as far as our relationship was concerned.

When you make a mistake, somebody has to be there to help you. And that's part of people serving others. It's the same as when Jesus healed the guard's ear after the ear cutting episode. After the resurrection, Peter finally had the chance to talk to Jesus again when they were on the lakeshore. The significant thing is that Jesus didn't holler at him; He just gave Peter a higher vision of his calling. If I knew people with whom I worked were giving everything they had and they tripped up, my duty would be to help them back up.

Finding Their Place

Some people are just not happy because they don't have the talents, gifts, or preparation to do a job. If they aren't in the right position, then it's the leader's responsibility to help find a place for them where their gifts and talents can be better utilized.

Other people reach a place that's as high as they're capable of going at the time. You can't push these people further, or you would be doing a disservice to them. The time might not be right yet for them to advance—they might be too immature, or they might just be happy in what they're doing. You need to discern exactly where they are so you will know how to deal with them.

Then there are others that I call diamonds in the rough, with whom you can spend time and develop their gifts and their talents. These people grasp their opportunities with both hands and continue to progress from one position to another. The man who is president and CEO right now of Flowers Foods is a young man who went to work for us right out of high school. We saw great potential in him. He married his high school sweetheart and started working for Flowers Foods.

We began to see that he really had the gifts and talents to advance far. He couldn't afford to go to college, so we began to move him different places to give him a varied experience. We put him in different environments and situations from small towns to big cities. He quickly went up the ladder as we continually promoted him for his excellent performance. He is a tremendous Christian man, and as he progressed with the company, he handled the promotions well. He wasn't perfect, but he always handled things properly, and now he's a chief executive officer. He was not a power seeker, but used the gifts and talents God gave him and received power in return that he used for God's glory.

Insecure People Are Ineffective

Anywhere you go, you will have people pleasers and people that base their decisions on their own personal agenda based on their size, who they are, where they come from, their background and education. Their insecurity is manifested in different ways, but it's obvious they will need to work at it to become more effective. I know that it took me a while to really begin to feel secure in who I was and the responsibility I had at such a young age.

Over the years I have discovered that regardless of how smart you are, how much money you have, how good-looking you are, or what kind of car you drive, there's always somebody that's going to be better than you. And God's going to make it a point to bring them across your path. You have a choice: you either just don't worry about that type of thing, or you get bogged down in it. I think the further you advance, the less room there is to be intimidated.

When I was at Flowers, we attended American Baker's Association meetings where there were attendees who were managing companies two or three times as large as Flowers. I had to choose whether or not I would be intimidated by them. I had to realize that comparing myself to others was not the way. My confidence had to be who I was in the Lord. In effect, making a comparison is saying, "God, the giftings and callings that You've put in me are not enough." Changing this attitude is part of the transformation that goes on as you grow as a Christian.

There are many problems occurring in corporate America because of insecurity and the need to overcome it. In a lower level of management, you might see some people that are engaging in personal destructive activities to compensate for their insecurity. Another unfortunate problem that can stem from insecurity is when somebody begins to dictate to their employees, becoming like a little Hitler. This behavior reveals an insecure attitude that says, "Because you work for me, therefore, you have no way to respond to what I am saying to you. So I'm going to lord it over you." Eventually, however, when you advance to a certain level of management, most of those insecure people can't be found. You can't have insecure people as managers when you're trying to run the company competently.

There is probably some insecurity in all of us, to a certain extent. But I think that when you promote people within the company, those in upper management have already gained confidence in who they are and in their ability to do their job. They have successfully dealt with complicated issues over the years, which helps them feel secure in their ability to handle increasingly difficult ones.

Principles of Good Leadership

One of the key functions of leadership is to be

able to discern when someone is ready to handle more responsibility and not expect them to handle something that's too big for them. Management needs to be careful that they don't give the five talents to the guy that can only handle one. I saw that so clearly when I ran a plant years ago. There was a wrapping machine supervisor who, all his life, had wanted to supervise that wrapping machine. When he finally did, he was happy and made a good living, but he was satisfied with the position because he was a two talent guy. He was not looking to advance further. One thing we have to keep in mind is how valuable these kinds of people are to a company. We can't function properly without them.

Appreciating everyone and everything they're doing is a crucial key to understanding people and how a company works. The guy that's sweeping the floor at midnight is very important to the organization, as is the fellow that's checking the ingredients to be sure they adhere to the company's standards. You cannot realize this principle of valuing others if you have an arrogant, selfish attitude.

Going one step further and letting people know how much you value and appreciate them is also an important function of a leader. For example, I loved to go into the marketplace to check things out and meet our distributors. One day we were in the Orlando area and ran into one of them. As I talked with him, I learned how much his route was adding to the company's bottom line. He wasn't bragging; he was just telling me about it. Whenever I heard things like that, I would write to the employee. And so after I returned to the office, I wrote him a personal letter, telling him how much I enjoyed meeting him and how much we appreciated him in the company. I found out later that he framed the letter and put it in his living room.

Another practice we followed was to send birthday cards to the employees. I signed every one that I sent and wrote a special note to the ones I personally knew. Going that little extra distance to say you really appreciate what they're doing brings a higher level of performance and excellence to a company.

I liked to talk to people in the plants, and I would ask them about their families. When you ask that question, you better be ready for any kind of answer. You may learn about a wife that just left with another man or about someone's daughter who is not doing well. I'd make mental notes of what I was told and many times I'd later go back in the plant and ask the employee some specific question dealing with their situation. That is not hard to do, but it means so much to the employees.

One day I was talking with a fellow who was running one of our plants. When I found out his daughter was being stalked, I told him, "Let's see what your legal rights are; let's get a detective; let's get the police involved." I went that extra step. Years later, he said he would never forget how I helped him with that situation. Small things like that make a significant difference.

Another time I was in Atlanta, and I was in one of the plants, inspecting a big freezer with an employee. A friend of his had just died, and he had been asked to speak at the funeral. In the course of conversation, he asked me what I thought he should say. He and I talked about it for about 20 minutes. Later he told me how much it meant that I had spent that time with him.

Does it make any money or show up on the bottom line tomorrow when you do things like this today? No. Does it show up on the bottom line ten years from now? Quite possibly. It definitely shows up in the lives you touch.

CHAPTER EIGHT

Finances and the Christian

Let's talk about money. There is nothing wrong with money or having a new car or a nice home. The problem arises when we start to love money so much that we turn our possessions into idols. And we make a big mistake when we start believing our income is a product solely of our efforts.

Another problem is when people suddenly get into a position where they are entrusted to spend the company's money to buy goods, services, or resources. If they're not careful, they can get confused knowing whether it's company money or their money that they're spending. A further problem occurs when vendors begin to cater to employees and puff them up. It's the type of thing you see screaming across the headlines about corporate America. Some large vendors take people on trips, for example, to ensure their sales, but it can also happen on a much lower scale and still be the same thing. For example, let's say you buy gas from two suppliers and one of them brings you a box of candy. If you let that affect who you purchase the gas from and not use your company's guidelines, then the vendor is working on your pride, making you feel more powerful.

I spent two years in Washington D.C. as the chairman of the American Baker's Association. We would visit senators and congressmen about a farm bill, for instance, and try to make our case based on concrete evidence. Obviously, we had a pact that we would contribute to their elections, but it was all done following the law's guidelines. I never tried to work on a guy's ego, I guess I was naïve enough to believe that they didn't do that, but it was obvious that many of them did.

Acquiring Wealth

Several years ago, I was speaking about leadership skills to a group of pastors. One fellow came up to me, handed me a dollar bill and said, "I was praying for you this morning, and the Lord told me to give you all of the money I had on me." He added that God had told him I was supposed to sell everything that I had and give it to the poor.

This might sound a little convenient, but I don't think I have to impoverish myself in order to serve the Lord. I just don't subscribe to the philosophy that having money is a barrier to service. It's our whole attitude toward money that's important. Money can either master you or you can master it, but the only way you are going to master money is to allow Jesus Christ to master you.

There are plenty of rich people in the Bible. The Old Testament is full of them. For example, Jesus and the disciples shared the Last Supper in the upper room. Somebody had to have had the money to build the two-story house, and Jesus never said that this person was wrong for doing it.

One of the problems with having money is that we tend to think we don't need anything or anyone else. Why do any of us need Jesus when we are at the helm of a company and everyone is catering to us? What do we need when we are leaving others in the dust as we climb the ladder of success? When we're nearing the top level, everybody wants to wine and dine us.

In America, many of us are very blessed from a material standpoint. But eventually the trappings of success—the fancy cars, the frequent travel, the wining and dining, and all of that money—aren't going to be enough. It's human nature to want more of everything, but the simple truth is that if we're not satisfied with what we have now, we'll never be satisfied with what we get in the future. And that holds true whether we're at the top or the bottom of the earning curve. Too often, those who do not have something bigger than themselves to turn to end up turning to alcohol or drugs or engage in other self-destructive activities.

There's a passage in the Old Testament book Ecclesiastes that talks about the futility of depending on our wealth for everything. It reads:

> *How absurd to think that wealth brings true happiness! The more you have, the more people come to help you spend it. So what is the advantage of wealth—except perhaps to watch it run through your fingers? People who work hard sleep well, whether they eat little or much. But the rich are always worrying and seldom get a good night's sleep.... Riches are sometimes hoarded to the harm of the saver; or they are put into risky investments that turn sour and everything is lost. People who live only for wealth come to the end of their lives as naked and empty-handed as on the day they were born* (Eccl. 5:10-15).

I have no idea where Bill Gates stands with regard to God, but he seems to understand that all those billions and billions of dollars are not his alone. Yes, he's obviously enjoying his wealth. But he's also set up a multi-billion dollar foundation that provides vaccinations for children in Third World countries. Whether he knows it or not, he is putting his wealth into service for God. Now that's success. If all Christians gave their tithe, the world would be a different place; so much suffering could be eliminated and so many government programs would be unnecessary.

Learning How to Handle Finances

Often somebody's promotion brings them to a point where they are making more money than they have ever made in their lives. Money is an awesome responsibility, particularly if you have surplus money. The question becomes, what are you going to do with it? Whether it's a dollar or it's $10 million, in God's eyes, it doesn't matter. If I have an extra dollar, what I do with that extra dollar and how I deal with it is important. And it's the same principle as somebody with $10 million. How you deal with this situation is an important responsibility. So many superstars and lottery winners obtain a lot of money and then they throw it away because they don't know how to handle it.

We need to realize that every asset we have is not ours; we are only stewards of it, just as we are stewards of our kids when we were raising them. Jacqueline and I have been very blessed and we enjoy helping people, but that could become prideful if we think, *Look at what we're doing for the less fortunate.* I think the reason that God says to bless others quietly is because we can get puffed up when we give to others.

I was on a plane one time and engaged in a conversation with a fellow who was sitting next to me. He was a businessman from Arkansas who was going to Mexico with his church to take over the administration of a hospital. He was walking away from everything to serve God in Mexico. He had been to Washington, visiting different churches and trying to raise his support. He was a fine Christian. I enjoyed talking to him and the Lord spoke to me, "Give this man this much money." I said, "Lord, I don't believe I'm hearing what You are saying." We were landing in Atlanta, and I felt strongly that I needed to write him a check. I pulled one out and wrote it for the amount of money God had told me to write. As we were walking off the plane, I handed it to him and disappeared in the crowd. And I thought, *Well, I'll never hear from this guy again.*

About three days later, I received a letter from the man (I had my address on the check), and he wrote, "The amount you gave me was the exact amount that I needed to complete my move to go to Mexico." That made me cheerful, not cheerful from a bragging standpoint or from a "look what I've done, let me put it on the front page of the paper" standpoint. It was between God and me. It's not the amount we give; it's about being obedient when God says to do it. Just like the widow that gave all she had. The issue is what is going on as far as our hearts. We need to continue to grow in understanding that we are simply stewards of what God has given us.

Reaping the Benefits

Is there a connection between our giving and our prospering? That idea has been often abused in Christianity. I've been in all different kinds of churches where offerings were taken. Some say that if you give $50, God will give you back $500. Unfortunately, the motivation so often has been "give to get back more." I think the attitude of the heart is what is important when you give. We do not need to expect to be repaid since we are only stewards of what God has given us. On the other hand, because of God's law of sowing and reaping, God will bless us in return in many ways, not just in money. There will be a lot of things that will change for your benefit when you give. I think once I became a Christian and began to give of myself and also my finances, God restored relationships in my life.

One time I had a situation in which I was involved in a dispute with an individual over some money. Although I was a Christian, I came down real strong on him about it. I finally began to see I was wrong because I was looking at the money from a standpoint of something that I possessed. I finally went back to the individual, and we worked it out and I asked for forgiveness. The following Christmas was one of the best holidays we had ever had with one of our sons, although he had nothing whatsoever to do with the dispute. I'm not saying that if I hadn't done that we wouldn't have had that experience, but it certainly cleared the air. When you walk carefully in God's ways, it's amazing what it does for you. I had baggage that I was carrying because I was upset and unforgiving. But when I finally realized what was happening and got it all worked out, it made a difference in my attitude toward other people.

We are stewards of what God has entrusted us. It all belongs to Him. At the end of the day, when our time comes to go be with the Lord, we can't carry it with us.

It's All God's

At times, I've had an unnecessary guilt trip about things I have purchased. After I became a Christian, for example, I bought the farm in Pavo. At first I wasn't sure if I was allowed to enjoy it, but I eventually saw it as an investment. I decided to figure out how to make the land productive. I planted trees, irrigation systems, and the value has gone up tremendously because of that approach to it. It's the same with our beach condo. We bought it about five or six years ago, and we'll be able to sell it at an increased value. And once again we will pray about what we do with this money.

Jesus doesn't tell us all to do the same thing. He told the rich young ruler to give away everything. In another instance, when the tax collector said he would give away half of his money, Jesus never told him to give it all away, probably because the tax collector's heart was right. The whole area of money comes back to a heart issue. Abraham, Joseph, Moses—these people all had money. Even Jesus and His disciples did.

Our value system needs to be based on God's Word and what He says. Love the Lord your God with all your heart, with all your soul, and all your mind. And as you do that, all these other things begin to take second place. But on top of that, the talents, gifting and callings you have grow right along with it, and the money follows.

God says that He trusts us to continue to sow into His kingdom with our money. There's nothing wrong with living in a nice house. On the other hand, when our attitude toward money is right, we don't need more in order to feel content. It's just like driving my car—I'm not trying to make a statement by driving a car with 100,000 miles on it. I like that car and don't have any reason to get another one. People have said to me, "Hey, why don't you buy one of these new ones? You can afford it." I always reply, "I don't want a new car, I'm happy with what I have." I'm not self-righteous; I'm just content with what I already have.

Get Rich Quick

Get rich quick schemes have devastated many Christians. Several years ago, a young man who was in our church came to me and said, "Heeth, there's a trillion, not a billion, a trillion dollars in a bank in Switzerland, and they need another $50-60,000 for lawyer fees to break it loose. I'm going to invest $10,000 and in return, I'll receive several million dollars. He said the Lord told him and his wife to do this. And then he asked me what I thought about it. I told him that I'd be very frank with him—he missed God because it just was not going to work that way. He became upset with me. To make a long story short, he ended up losing all his money along with his marriage.

I think that so often what happens with these get rich quick schemes is that it preys on a person's greed factor. "Look at what I can get, and I don't really have to go and work for it." People want to make a killing; they want to do it quickly and not the slow, sure way. There have been some people who actually have made a fortune quickly, such as in the future's market, buying options. There is a way you can jump in to the market and make a quick buck, but you better know what you are doing. There are not many people who can do it. There have been people who have made killings in real estate by being in the right place at the right time. Several years ago you could have bought $100,000 worth of beachfront property that might be worth a million dollars today. Risk goes with this kind of investment, but a person that is skilled in real estate and uses it to make a pile of money is reaping from his knowledge, skills, and talent. It's not the route that the average person can take.

I come from a school that says get rich quick things are mainly schemes to get someone else rich. Becoming wealthy is usually a day-in and day-out process whereby you continue to grow and mature while having the right attitude about money. Money is either going to run you, or God's going to run you and you'll run the money. But the only way you are going to run the money is to have a close relationship with the Lord.

CHAPTER NINE

The Challenge of Excellence

When I was in military school, we used to spit-shine our boots until you could see yourself in them. To get into our uniforms, we'd have to stand on a chair because we wanted to keep that straight crease. We looked great on the outside, but that had nothing to do with what we were like inside.

It's like inspecting our food plants for good sanitation. When we entered them, we could look at the machinery, the walls, and the floors, and it would be spotless. But then if we'd open the closets, pull the guards off some of the motors and take off some of the panels and look behind them,

118

we might see things that we didn't want to see. Yet we had a reputation for having the cleanest plants in the industry. What God is desiring is that we are clean on both the inside and the outside.

As soon as some people become Christians, they immediately shine their shoes, put on their pants with the straight crease and the starched shirt, and fix their tie just right, but they still have the same problems because the process of becoming Christ-like takes time. You just can't do it overnight. After a big evangelistic crusade, only a small percentage of those who made a decision for Christ remain Christians because they based their decision on something emotional. After two, three, or four weeks, they begin to ask, "How come I'm still having problems?" They don't realize it's an internal process that must take place.

In my experience in the business world, I met many people, from politicians to owners of bakeries to supermarket executives. You don't begin a relationship with them by quoting the scriptures. You let them get to know you as who you are and what you are. I was very fortunate to have many good relationships with people in the industry who were Christians. But they didn't walk around with a sign on them that read, "I'm a Christian." How you conduct yourself eventually identifies you as a Christian.

I became good friends with the owner of a big

chain in east Texas who was a good customer. We went hunting together, and it's amazing when you spend time with an individual away from the business how you get to really know them. That's how I came to know him as a Christian.

The Lord will bring along people in the marketplace to help you if you really want to serve Him, be obedient, and try to live by His commandments. You might think it's a lonely world out there in that respect, but it's really not. There are many, fine Christian men and women out there in the marketplace, and you will eventually begin to know who they are. When we attended American Baker's Association meetings to discuss generic issues pertinent to the industry, it didn't take long before I knew some of them were Christians. I began to meet the ones who were really dedicated and wanted to go on with the Lord.

It's not easy to be a vibrant Christian in the marketplace because Satan's real, and it's just a matter of when and how you will be tempted. Satan knows where you are most vulnerable. The only ways to defeat the temptations he brings are to pray, read the Bible, read Christian books, and be around godly people like those I've talked about whom God brings across your path.

When you're involved with people that are not walking close to God, you can pray for them silently and look at them as people whom God loves. If you pray that God will help you to be used in any way in someone's life, then the opportunities will come along. It took me a while to gain enough boldness to share with others when I recognized the opportunity. One time when we were at a meeting in Phoenix, one of the head guys at a big supplier of Flowers and I became friends. We were just talking and suddenly God opened the door for me to start sharing with him. The next thing I knew we were up in my room, had the Bible out, and we were talking about it. We need to be sensitive when opportunities present themselves. If we try and make our own opportunity, usually the anointing is not there. But when God goes ahead of us, we can confidently share with others what God has done for us.

Through the years I have seen that when a person is honest and transparent, it really opens other people up. Sincerity is something you can really feel. So often in the marketplace and the business world, we have to always put our best foot forward in dealing with profit and loss statements, finances, advertising, and plant facilities. Many times we don't take the time to get to know those around us and find out what's going on in their lives. We need to ask God for the discernment to know when the time is right.

Making Decisions

We cannot compromise our principles, ethics, character or our walk with God in our decision making process in business. One Old Testament figure—Daniel—comes to mind. Daniel was the brightest of the bright and was chosen from among the captured nobility to be educated in the Babylonian culture. Although this education taught him how to handle himself in their world, he never compromised his relationship with God. Above all, he sought God's guidance and protection in prayer.

As a result, God's favor was upon him and the king planned to set him over the entire kingdom. When the other government officials heard of this, they were jealous and sought to bring charges against him, but could find no corruption in him. They knew of his love for God and set a trap for him by having the king declare that people could only pray to the king for the next 30 days. Of course that only caused Daniel to pray more fervently to his God, and he was thrown in the lions' den as a result.

After a sleepless night, the king hurried to the lions' den and called out to Daniel, "Daniel, servant of the living God, has your God, whom you serve continually, been able to rescue you from the lions?" (Daniel 6:6) After seeing what God had done for Daniel, the king issued a decree that people must fear and reverence the God of Daniel. What a victorious result from a potentially dangerous decision that Daniel had made!

Now our business decisions do not usually have the possibility of our being thrown to the lions if we make a mistake (although I am sure in some companies it might feel like it). But the story illustrates the fact that we need to seek God in all our decisions. If we needed to make a decision to build a new plant at Flowers, for example, and we were going to put out millions to do so, we had to cautiously weigh various aspects of the package before proceeding. We had to decide, first of all, whether or not we actually needed it from a production standpoint, where the finances would come from, and if we would receive an appropriate return on our money through better productivity. At this point our team people, our accounting people and our engineers helped us sift through all the options. In the meantime, I always prayed silently for the Lord to help us and guide us through our meeting.

We must be careful about our decisions because there are so many people who will be affected by them. We need to do a lot of praying, which helps to bring that peace that surpasses all understanding. That peace does not come overnight, and you don't always have it everyday. That's just the way it is. The one way to increase your peace is to develop a closer relationship with the Lord.

Paul went through beatings in jail, snake bites, shipwrecks, and false accusations. But the man sang in jail. I've often wondered how he could do it. If that had been me 2,000 years ago, it would have been very difficult to sing in the midst of such persecution. What the man had going for him was a relationship with the Lord. He had heard what God's mission was for him, and he pursued it with much prayer. As a result, he knew that he was on course and what he was doing was right.

Being Faithful

There are many biblical figures from whom we can learn a great deal about wise living, which always results in excellence. These people were faithful to God in extraordinarily difficult circumstances. They were overcomers.

Again we look to Joseph who was such a man. Joseph was successful wherever he landed. Joseph wanted to please God, and God was with him. Joseph continued to pursue excellence when his life was not going in the direction he expected. He never failed to live up to the high standards even when he was treated unjustly.

God watched over Joseph and continued to

bless him as he served as a slave in Potiphar's house. He gave Joseph success in everything he did, which did not go unnoticed by Potiphar. Joseph became one of Potiphar's favorites and soon was put in charge of his entire household and all his business dealings. For Joseph's sake, from the day he assumed a management position, God began to also bless Potiphar. All his household affairs began to run smoothly, and his crops and livestock flourished. Eventually Potiphar gave Joseph complete administrative responsibility over everything he owned.

Things went well until Potiphar's wife took a liking to Joseph. She tried to seduce him, and, when he turned down her sexual advances, she told Potiphar that Joseph had attempted to rape her. Understandably, Potiphar was furious with Joseph and threw him into prison. It wasn't long, however, before the chief jailer put Joseph in charge of all the other prisoners and over everything that happened in the prison. "The chief jailer had no more worries after that, because Joseph took care of everything. The Lord was with him making everything run smoothly and successfully" (Gen. 39:21-23).

Some time later, Pharaoh's chief cup-bearer and chief baker offended him and he put them in the prison where Joseph was being held. Potiphar assigned Joseph to take care of them. One night both the cup-bearer and the baker had dreams.

They sought out Joseph to tell them the meaning of the dreams. Explaining that God, not he, was doing the interpreting, Joseph delivered good news and bad. In three days the cup-bearer would return to Pharaoh's good favor, Joseph said, and the baker would be beheaded. Joseph asked the cup-bearer to put in a good word for him with Pharaoh when he returned to his duties.

When the cup-bearer was summoned back into service for Pharaoh's birthday, he forgot all about Joseph. It wasn't until two years later, when Pharaoh needed a dream interpreted, that the cup-bearer remembered Joseph. Upon hearing of Joseph's abilities, Pharaoh immediately sent for him.

Joseph told Pharaoh that Egypt soon would experience seven years of prosperity, which would be followed by seven years of famine. He suggested that Pharaoh appoint the wisest man in Egypt to coordinate a nationwide program of crop collection and storage so that there would be enough to eat when the seven years of famine came.

If you were in Pharaoh's shoes, whom would you have been appointed to direct the project? Pharaoh chose Joseph, even though he was just a Jewish slave. At age 30, Joseph took charge of the entire land of Egypt. Eventually, Joseph's father, Jacob, and all of his descendents joined him there, where they were assigned the best land of the country. Joseph remained in Egypt until his death at the age of 110.

In Joseph, we have a man of principles, a man of vision. He was a young person who was betrayed by his insanely jealous brothers and sold into slavery—to the reviled Egyptians, no less. He was alone in his faith. Yet he never stopped believing in God or giving Him the credit. He never gave into temptation nor ceased to live up to the highest standards, even when he was treated unjustly.

Faced with a daunting challenge of the coming famine that God had revealed to him, Joseph developed a plan to save the Egyptian people from starvation. In all likelihood, this Jewish slave was held in higher esteem by the Egyptians than most of their own. Surely some of them saw something different in him.

Despite what his brothers had done to him, Joseph never stopped loving them. When he finally had the opportunity to confront them, his response was magnificent. "God turned into good what you meant for evil" (Gen. 50:19-20). That one sentence should be etched on the desktop of every CEO in America. If we are faithful to Him, God will do the same for us.

Wise Living

How does this apply to us today? As Christians in the marketplace, we are faced daily with choices and trials, temptations and adversity. When we are faithful to God's value system, we will learn to recognize evil and turn from it.

Jesus sets the standard, not man. When we judge ourselves, or others judge us by worldly standards, we can miss the fact that we are drifting off course. This can lead to unbridled pride and a selfish, conceited attitude. I found myself in just such a situation in the 1980s, when Flowers experienced great company growth, increased profits, and national recognition. Flowers was regarded as one of the best in the industry, a fact that we were quite proud of. And I was president of the American Bakers' Association, which represents the bakeries in the United States.

Just when I thought everything was just as it should be, Jacqueline, in the nicest possible way, let me know that I was becoming prideful and arrogant, not exactly the attitude that furthers us in our walk with Jesus. As a friend of mine, Bishop Bill Hamon says, unguarded strength can become a double weakness. I saw that I needed to adjust my mindset, and that took me right back to Jesus Christ.

We must continually give careful study to the life of Jesus. When pressure comes, it is often difficult to recognize the correct thing to do. We aren't alone in this. Giants of the Bible also had this problem. Adam disobeyed God by eating the fruit. Abraham lied to Pharaoh. Moses became angry. David committed adultery and murder. Peter denied Jesus. The list goes on and on. In today's world we are often faced with many of the same issues as did these giants of the faith. We may justify what we do by asking ourselves and others, "Did God really say that?"

Like Abraham who lied to Pharaoh, we are sometimes tempted to bend the truth rather than face the reality of the situation. Like Moses with the rock, anger is something we all must struggle with. These temptations to stray from God's direction, whether due to fear or anger, must be overcome by faith so that they do not become sin.

So often, human knowledge can work against our faith and value system, just as the Babylonian teaching must have presented a challenge to Daniel. In Ephesians 5:15-16, written 2,000 years ago, Paul cautions us to be careful how we live, "...not as fools, but as those who are wise. Make the most of every opportunity in these evil days." We need the same sense of urgency today because we, too, face evil.

So how do we go about making significant decisions? We need to get as much of the necessary information as we can but also realize we're never going to have it all because unexpected things will always come along. After we assemble the information, we can go before the Lord and say, "Lord, we've done our homework on this thing, now we need Your guidance and peace to make the right decision." Once we do that, we need to recognize the fact that we might fail. Many Christians will have a hard time with that. The key is to know that even when we make a wrong decision, we do not have to stay down but we can get back up, adjust our course, and continue to pursue our vision.

I remember one particular time we bought two bakeries in Virginia. The day we started to operate this new venture, Murphy's law took over—whatever could go wrong did go wrong. Now that wasn't in the game plan, but we said, "Okay, we've made the decision, now let's make it work." As a result, within the next few months we had a smooth running operation.

The question arises, "How do you know if the answer you receive to your prayer comes out of your own desire to succeed or it's really the Lord speaking to you?" Well, you need to have other people around too who can bring you information and stand with you in prayer. You're not on an island by yourself out there. Paul first had Barnabas and then Timothy with him. We are strengthened and encouraged when we walk together with others in God's family.

Walking the Christian life is not complicated. The difficulty lies in staying on course when things are not going our way.

As Christians in the marketplace, we all find ourselves faced with trials and temptations. We learn the true depth of our character in how we react under pressure. In the face of overwhelming pressure—rejection, slander, abandonment, misunderstanding and much disappointment—Joseph did not compromise his godly value system. By successfully overcoming adversity, he gained maturity and a strong character. We learn the depth of our character in how we respond under pressure. The challenge of excellence is a high call that God has for us in the marketplace.

CHAPTER TEN

A Call to the Cross

It should be obvious by now that I believe our relationship with God is an intrinsic part of our fulfilling a call to excellence. One obstacle to knowing God is our need for irrefutable proof that God exists. When I first began studying about Jesus, I wanted someone to prove His existence to me from an historical standpoint. I wanted something tangible that I could put my hands around. After struggling mightily with this, I came to the realization that, at some point, we have to step out in faith. We can spend the rest of our lives asking, "Where's the proof?" or we can look around us at all that He created and say, "I believe."

Our highest purpose in life is to know God. God loves us more than we can imagine. The more we know about Him, the greater our capacity to love Him. Before we become Christians, we live in the darkness that comes from not knowing Him.

Knowing God

Sometimes even before we know that God is God, we hear a voice calling out to us from the void. God is awesome. He's also available. You don't need to go through an appointment secretary to get in to see Him. You don't need to know the secret handshake. You can stop right now, in the middle of this sentence, and talk to God. He is with you at this very moment. "But I don't know what to say!" you may be thinking. No problem. Just speak from your heart. You don't have to be Billy Graham or the chief toastmaster to talk to the Lord. Talk to Him as if He were your best friend. After all, He is.

What you say to God is between you and Him. You can tell Him anything. (Like it or not, He knows it anyway!) You know He will keep your conversations confidential. You can share your greatest doubts, your biggest fears, your triumphs and your joys. You can laugh; you can cry. You can share a moment of silence. I believe that He wants us to share everything with Him. There is no right or wrong way to talk with God. Some people believe that it is wrong to bring our minor concerns to Him. After all, He is dealing with wars, famine and disease. My personal belief is that no concern is too small, "for He created us and knows every hair on our heads" (Luke 12:7).

Last spring, I watched a pair of doves over the course of a number of weeks as I had my morning coffee on our back porch. The first day I noticed them, they made numerous trips back and forth from the roof, bringing bits of pine straw to reinforce an old nest they had spotted in a nearby camellia bush. After the female laid her eggs, I watched her sit on that nest for hours on end. Some days it rained as if it never would stop. Still, she persevered.

After the chicks hatched, I watched the new parents bring them food. After a week or so, the chicks began to create quite a stir as they cried for more, with their little heads bobbing up over the top of the nest and their yellow beaks outstretched. I found the racket comforting, knowing that they had survived another night.

I believe that it's like that with God. Just as I watched that little family of birds, God intently watches us. He notices the little things; nothing escapes His gaze. He loves us.

Hearing God

We get to know God by reading the Bible. When I worked for Flowers, I tried to spend an hour every morning to read the Bible. I still try to read it every day. When I don't read it for some reason, my day doesn't feel right.

The Bible is my rudder. It has seen me through some pretty heavy times. In my experience, it's one of the best ways to hear from God. Whatever it takes, we have to start reading. A good starting point is the four gospels—Matthew, Mark, Luke and John—eyewitness accounts of Jesus' itinerant ministry, death, and resurrection. You don't need to attend seminary to understand what's written there. The key to reading the Bible is that we read it from the standpoint of asking what it is that God has to say to us through it.

We all have a call and a purpose for our lives. Before we were conceived in our mother's womb, God had something in mind for us to do. "For we are His masterpiece. He has created us anew in Christ Jesus so that we can do the good things He planned for us long ago" (Eph. 2:10).

One of the people who heard God's voice and responded to His call was Mother Teresa. When she was a little girl in Albania, she probably looked like any other child. Yet she made an extraordinary difference in the lives of millions of people in India and around the world through her willingness to trust God to give her the tools she needed to walk in His will.

Imagine the sea of people that churns in Calcutta's poorest neighborhoods. Imagine the overwhelming need for food, for medical attention, for hope. Imagine that you don't speak the language or know the culture. Imagine that you may be the only Christian among tens of millions of non-believers. Imagine that you are alone in reaching out to people who are defeated, who come to life without the slightest indication that they matter to someone or that their lives have value.

Mother Teresa could have turned and run from that deep well of suffering, but she didn't. A missionary who spent the day with her at one of her missions in India was impressed with the size of her hands. They were disproportionately large for her tiny body, she said. Yet they were a powerful symbol of her willingness to serve.

Very few of us are going to get the call to serve so great a need. But we all have been given assignments. We learn to hear God's voice by spending time with Him. Nowadays, there is so much "noise" in our lives that it is often difficult to hear His voice above the din. By noise, I don't mean just the sounds that we hear—and there are plenty of them. I'm talking about the things that we accumulate to the point that we are about to drown in them—the busy work, for example, or the constant rush to transport our kids to their next activity. When we can't even hear ourselves think, it should come as no surprise that we are having difficulty hearing God.

The Refiner's Fire

It's easy to have faith during the good times. But if there is a guarantee in life, it is that our faith will be tested. It might be the illness or death of a loved one or the senseless loss of life caused by a natural disaster or a terrorist attack. When things are at their worst, we believers face the refiner's fire. Peter cautions us,

> *Be careful! Watch out for attacks from the devil, your great enemy. He prowls around like some roaring lion, looking for some victim to devour. Take a firm stance against him and be strong in your faith* (1 Peter 5:8-9).

Non-believers often challenge the faithful by questioning how we can believe in God when there is so much cruelty, pain, and suffering in the world. The fact is that God has the power to diffuse the most powerful bomb, to cure the terminally ill, to strike dead anyone who would bring harm to any of His children. He could have saved Jesus from crucifixion. But then everything would be different.

From the very beginning in the Garden of Eden, God has given mankind free will. Adam chose to take a bite from the apple. That turned out to be a bad choice. More recently, suicide bombers have taken thousands of innocent lives in an attempt to martyr themselves and further their political cause. Those were horrible choices. In short, today's high-risk world is of our own making, the end product of our cumulative choices.

Our confidence in God's ability to save us is not based on any prior guarantee of deliverance. Neither is our worship. When we proclaim our faith, we are not testing God's faithfulness to us or whether He is deserving of our faith and service.

While I am trying mightily to live the life that God wants for me, I know that I am very much a work in progress. So are we all. I don't mean to say that I have already achieved these things or that I have already reached perfection! But I keep working toward that day when I will finally be all that Christ Jesus saved me for and wants me to be.

> *No...I am not all I should be, but I am focusing all my energies on this one thing: Forgetting the past and looking forward to what lies ahead, I strain to reach the end of the race and receive the prize for which God, through Christ Jesus, is calling us up to heaven* (Phil. 3:13-14).

Meaning of Life

Nearly 3,000 years ago, King Solomon pondered the age-old question, "What is the meaning of life?" His writing, captured in Ecclesiastes in the Old Testament, looks at life from the perspective of an immensely wise, fabulously wealthy, and politically powerful individual. Solomon writes of the futility of wisdom, pleasure, work, political power and wealth. He concludes that life is utterly meaningless apart from knowing, worshiping and obeying God.

> *Here is my final conclusion. Fear God and obey His commands, for this is the duty of every person. God will judge us for everything we do, including every secret thing, whether good or bad* (Eccl. 12:13-14).

Why is it that some people view the Ten Commandments as archaic, as part of some ancient code of conduct? Why is it that they view the Ten Commandments as too religious to post in public places or teach in public schools? Aren't they just common sense? Aren't they the prescription for happiness and good living? Shouldn't we thank God for keeping it simple? It's humankind that complicates things. The Ten Commandments are the cornerstones of civilization. Given where we are today as a society, it is absolutely impossible to imagine what life would be like if the Ten Commandments were never broken.

One Transcendent Truth

I have been in the marketplace for 40 years, 32 of them as a Christian. I can tell you that fearing God and obeying His commands is a tall order for anyone. It is a never ceasing struggle, regardless of our vocation. Through my experience, I've come to the conclusion that there are two fundamentals we must understand: the significance of the cross and the necessity of growing in our love and knowledge of Jesus Christ.

In his book, *The Cross Centered Life,* C.J. Mahaney notes that the Bible tells us while there are many different callings and many possible areas of service in the kingdom of God, "one transcendent truth should define our lives. One simple truth should motivate our work and affect every part of who we are: Christ died for our sins." As sinners, we would have no hope without the cross."

Throughout the New Testament, we are challenged to go after an intimate relationship with Christ. We are told that as we grow and mature in our love of Jesus, our love for each other will also grow. Just like everyone else, I have struggled with the command to love my neighbor as myself. None of us can achieve that attitude in the absence of God's grace. Unless we fill up with high-octane Christian love, we'll never be in a position to truly love our family, neighbors or co-workers.

God wants us to walk in peace and joy. He wants us to fulfill our destiny and call that He has on our life. He's standing at the pump ready to fill us up.

The time and energy we invest in knowing and loving God has a return that we cannot imagine. So how do we know that we are growing in our love and intimacy with God? "Examine yourselves to see if your faith is really genuine. Test yourselves. If you cannot tell that Jesus Christ is among you, it means you have failed the test" (2 Cor. 13:5).

We are constantly tested in our vocations. Our performance is reviewed. How are we doing? What do we need to do to improve our performance? When is our next promotion coming? In the marketplace, we turn to our boss for answers. If we own our own business, we look at the profit and loss statement. As Christians, the acid test is our desire to obey His Word and to live our lives as Jesus wants us to.

As a nation and as a society, we are results oriented. Over the past 32 years, I have been on a mission looking for results in my life that are Jesus-based. No, I haven't arrived. And that's what the cross is all about. There is no condemnation for those who are in Christ Jesus. When it comes to our Christian walk, we are either going forward or backward. There is no middle ground of

standing still. As Christians we are motivated to
grow and learn. His power and direction in our
lives always should be on the rise.

Having said that, we all will continue to face
trials. That's the nature of the role of Christians in
the marketplace.

> *These trials are only to test your faith to show
> that it is strong and pure. It is being tested as
> fire tests and purifies gold and your faith is
> far more precious to God than mere gold. So if
> your faith remains strong after being tried by
> fiery trials, it will bring you much praise and
> glory and honor on the day when Jesus Christ
> is revealed to the whole world* (1 Peter 1:7).

In the marketplace, unproductive, ineffective
people, plants, systems, and procedures aren't tol-
erated. They are either improved or new ones are
put in place. So why do we often tolerate this in-
consistency in our walk with God? Deeds do not
save us. Grace does. However, deeds based on
Christ's character are important. If we refuse to
follow God and instead follow our own selfish desires, we become enslaved to them. If we submit
our lives to Christ, He will free us from slavery to
sin.

We should all desire to live a life that is
pleasing to God. This cannot be done by living a
life of legalism—do's and don'ts. We'd be so busy
trying to keep up with the rules that we'd never

get in the game. Our journey of excellence is founded on moral purity in action.

At the end of our journey we will then receive that most valued of all accolades of success—our Lord and Saviour saying to us, "Well done, my good and faithful servant. Come and share your master's happiness."

Being a Christian isn't only a destination, it's also a journey that begins the day you turn your life over to God—the moment you are saved. My journey continues today. Every day, I step out in faith that I will break down any barrier that would keep me from responding to God's call on my life.

AFTERWORD

Even though we will never reach perfection in this life the Apostle Paul encourages us to press on to the upward call. As I have continued on in this journey I have found nine scriptures that are especially helpful to me. They are:

Matthew 22:37-38 – Jesus replied: "Love the Lord your God with all your heart and with all your soul and with all your mind." This is the first and greatest commandment.

I John 2:3 – We know that we have come to know him if we obey his commands.

Psalm 24:1 – The earth is the Lord's, and everything in it, the world, and all who live in it.

I John 2:15-16 – Do not love the world or anything in the world. If anyone loves the world, the love of the Father is not in him. For everything in the world – the cravings of sinful man, the lust of his eyes and the boasting of what he has and does- comes not from the Father but from the world.

Matthew 6:14-15 – For if you forgive men when they sin against you, your heavenly Father will also forgive you. But if you do not forgive men their sins, your Father will not forgive your sins.

Colossians 3:23 – Whatever you do, work at it with all your heart, as working for the Lord, not for men.

I Timothy 6:10 – For the love of money is a root of all kinds of evil. Some people, eager for money, have wandered from the faith and pierced themselves with many griefs.

Ephesians 5:25 – Husbands, love your wives, just as Christ loved the church and gave himself up for her.

Ephesians 6:4 - Fathers, do not exasperate your children; instead, bring them up in the training and instruction of the Lord.

About the Author

Heeth Varnedoe is a native and current resident of Thomasville, Georgia. After graduating from the University of Georgia, Heeth began his career with Flowers Foods, which spanned a total of 40 years. Upon his college graduation, he joined Flowers full time and was sent to Jacksonville, Florida as a route salesman. Through the years, Heeth took on additional responsibilities as the company grew. At his retirement, he was President and Chief Operating Officer of Flowers Foods, a Fortune 500 company.

Throughout his career, Heeth has been very active in the food industry. He has served as chairman of the American Bakers Association and on the ABA Board of Directors. He served two terms on the ABA Bakery Expo Committee. He also served on the Board of Trustees of the American Institute of Baking.

Heeth has been active in numerous civic activities. Heeth and Jacqueline are members of the New Covenant Church in Thomasville where Heeth serves as an elder, teaches classes on family relations, and is active in the men's ministry. He serves on the Board of Directors of Integrity

Media, the Board of Directors of Brett Chaffin's Outreach Ministries and is on the Board of Governors of Christian International.

During the last several years, Heeth and Jacqueline have traveled nationally and internationally ministering to various Christian groups.

Heeth and Jacqueline have been married for 46 years and have two married daughters, Jacqueline Morgan and Elizabeth Malone and two married sons, Heeth IV and Howard. They also have ten grandchildren.